JUST DELIVER
THE
MESSAGE

JUST DELIVER
THE
MESSAGE

LEANEAR RANDALL

ARPress
ILLUMINATING IDEAS.
EMPOWERING VOICES

ARPress
45 Dan Road Suite 5
Canton, MA 02021

Hotline: 1(888) 821-0229
Fax: 1(508) 545-7580

Ordering Information:
Quantity sales. Special discounts are available on quantity purchases by corporations, associations, and others. For details, contact the publisher at the address above.

Printed in the United States of America.

ISBN-13:	Softcover	979-8-89330-525-8
	eBook	979-8-89330-527-2
	Hardback	979-8-89330-526-5

Library of Congress Control Number: 2024900612

TABLE OF CONTENTS

CHAPTER 1

Thirty angry people, whose ages ranged from very young to elderly, both men and women alike with large piercing eyes yelled at a man bound at his ankles and wrists. "Hang him, hang him!" they demanded. "Kill the beast!" they screamed. Deep, inward anger adorned the sea of skewed faces, their eyes swelled, their lips twisted in oval pouched expressions, and their minds succumbed to unadul-terated hatred.

Demons and minions of darkness led by a greater demon indwelled their hosts. They became so excited that their twisted, ever-changing forms nearly burst into the physical realm. The demons' hosts began to pray to God, asking for his blessing while they continued their verbal insults. They sought God's permission to kill the bounded man. They sought the blessing of the Almighty God, but subliminally lusted for the great demon of the world of darkness. As the man dangled from the old oak tree, both young and old reveled in their unholy works. They would all be rewarded in time.

Bill Terry had listened to an inner voice that requested he remain calm. He shuffled across the dry grass being held upright by two burly men that were forcibly dragging him forward. What had he done to deserve this? Certainly, this mob had to be mistaken. His mind remained confused. Fear had initially overwhelmed him, but a mysterious feeling of serenity entered his being and calmed him. A bright, soothing image of calming light materialized as an enormous dominant figure in his mind, saying, *Fear not for you shall be together with the Almighty God very soon. Your unyielding faith in the Lord of Hosts has been rewarded. Soon you will be in his presence.*

Bill could not reconcile images that surfaced before him. Gone from his mind were the members of the bloodthirsty crowd, unabated fear, or finding reason at this time. His arms and feet were no longer bound as he stepped into a light of total serenity. Smiling faces of deceased family members and friends awaited him. He only knew freedom was all around.

An angel of God, like a stone of granite, stood defiantly before these minions of hell. "Be gone, you have no more reason to be here, your time grows short."

Red and black swirls of darkness began to materialize into human form, snickering as it formed. Many smaller acolytes sheep-ishly hid behind the folds in his robe. Their beady eyes appeared within the darkness surrounding him. "Today, I have claimed thirty new souls for my master," spoke the great demon, "and you have only one." He hissed as he laughed.

"In the name of Jesus," with a loud roaring voice, the angel spoke, "be gone!"

CHAPTER 2

Oklahoma City was riding a long NBA winning streak, which vaulted them into a first-place tie with the Houston Rockies. Being an Oklahoma City Lightening fan, and winning the game, Paul Lawrence was thrilled as the game clock flashed to zero. *Good game*, he thought. *All games are good when your favorite team wins.* He smiled.

Work came early in the morning, which caused Paul to pick up the remote from the chair's arm. His seeking finger fumbled for the Off button, which familiarity found quickly, and he turned the TV off. Silence immediately followed. *To bed*, he thought, cognizant of the time. *Tomorrow is going to be another busy day.* He turned the lights out and slowly made his way to his junky bedroom, which overlooked West Street in Old Town Alexandria. Countless times he had traversed this path in the dark, and he trusted the routine to avoid any incidents or unexpected mishaps with the furniture and his toes.

Rain was pounding heavily outside his window, and the sound resembled bullets slamming against a wall. *Pop, pop, pop.* The assaulting rain's arsenal splattered against the defensive windows. He flopped into bed, pulling the blanket over his head, slowly easing his nose from within to seek the unhindered air.

Paul tossed in his bed, backward and forward, simultaneously fumbling with the rough sheets. A thunderous flash of lightning pierced the ebony sky, creating a reoccurring battle between the light and dark. It raged violently and unchecked for seemingly forever, howling with crackling and bombardments of raindrops. Paul felt relieved that he was not an active participant struggling against the heavenly assault. His battle was far nearer, an active mind that carried on countless struggles that kept the solace of sleep at bay. Another loud *boom* and sleep remained elusive.

The sheets felt hard against his skin, and the bed lacked the soothing softness that gave comfort. Still, his mind remained totally awake, talking incessantly about numerous nonsensical thoughts that created countless emerging ideas, and none seemed to be eas-ily resolved. Not wanting to ease away from the bed that gave little comfort, he opened his eyes hoping that the time displaying from the nightstand on his smartwatch would reveal a welcome relief.

2:27 a.m., it glared. "Oh my God!" he said aloud. How long had he lingered following the game's end? Remembering everything now, his thoughts lingered on recollections of friends long gone from his life. In his mind, he would no longer establish a personal relation-ship with anyone; casual acquaintances were much better. He gave pause, Daniel, his lifelong blood brother, was different. *I would die for him.*

That darn watch even appears to be smiling. No relief. Another three plus hours of incessant torment. *Sleep, sleep, sleep.* A bullying strobe light heckled in his already troubled mind. He wanted to just get out of his bed and turn the TV on, but he knew that would only exacerbate this awake-sleep struggle. Maybe some "mother's little helpers" would tranquilize his mind and allow the respite of sleep to win the night. That would cause him to move. *No way am I going to rise from this bed and try to get back in it.* An old remedy surfaced in his mind, as he tossed and turned on his warm sheets enhanced by his nervous sweating. Inhale deeply…hold…release, inhale deeply…hold…release, inhale deeply… hold…and re…lea…se. Sleep appeared to overcome him.

Paul gazed into a dark and deceiving vastness without end. There prevailed a sense of hopelessness and lostness, a cloud of despair. He wanted to back up and run, but the heaviness of his mind weighed on him like a lead anvil. Sheer fear choked him into submission. *I need to scream! Where am I, and how did I get here? This is certainly an unknown reality. Wake up!* "wake up!" Paul shouted at the top of his lungs…but nothing happened.

A vague image of a clearing that lightened the area around him gave a better view of his surroundings. Paul wanted to back away but could not move. There was this endless road lurking off into a dull blackness. On either side of the road appeared a conflagration that illuminated countless faces that failed to burn; however, they cried out in unbroken agony, "Water…please, save me!" A deafness followed, interrupted only by the sound of weeping and gnashing of teeth.

Paul stood, spellbound. "Wake up!" he shouted to himself under his breath.

"Fear me, as you view your fate, for I am your salvation and your destiny. Worship me, and your plight may be reconsidered. Refuse, and join the sea of fire." Spittle sprayed out and immediately vaporized. The ephemeral image of the creature that burned crimson red swayed in the wind. "This may not be your destiny, because it is I that will determine your eternal fate. Praise me and live. Deny me and burn eternally," the creature chuckled. The Tormenter of Souls had been given great authority over the fallen. He reveled in his job, loathing the tormented as they sought refuge from their unending situation. A parade of souls arrived in clusters, frequently and unin-terrupted. They asked for mercy, but none came. Each receiving their just due.

Paul managed to say, "You lie! Who are you, and where am I?" "I have many names and are known by many more. Humans often know me as Al Lost, others call me Master, while others refer to me as the Commander. But what are titles between us? Worship me and live, earthly man! I could make it possible that you do not join your brothers," he said, snickering as he found it difficult to remain emotionless.

Paul again managed, "You lie," fighting tenaciously not to run away in fear. This abomination had engendered a ferocious, uncontrollable fear that threatened Paul's sanity. "This can only be a dream," he managed.

"Not only a dream, but your truth, and ultimate fate that awaits you due to juvenile denial," he snickered as the crimson glow brightened and faded. "Taste my rewards," he offered. Instantaneously, two beautiful scantily clad images appeared, suggesting that their beings were of a dubious nature.

Their hands sought to embrace his fear, but were held at bay. They moved to a new position, but still could not reach Paul. As he watched, filled with terror, they continuously sought him, but they were held back. Making no headway with Paul, they vanished.

"So, Paul, are you surprised that I know your name? What does your heart truly desire?" he murmured. "My Master said that you might be stubborn. An extended life, refrain from the eternal sea of weeping and gnashing of teeth, or richness and fame? Say it, my friend, and it will be yours." He sheepishly laughed. "I know your thoughts, and before you call his name, we will meet again and again."

"In the name of Jesus!" Paul cried loudly for help. Checking his watch, 2:30 a.m. flashed. Oh my God. Paul tugged the covers violently over his head. *That was a devilish nightmare and it seemed so real,* he thought. *What was that Bible verse against unholy struggle?* He fought with his mind to recollect the biblical verse to erase this mental abomination. His mouth was agape, fumbling with words torn from his mind. As suddenly as he proposed the question, it came in vivid clarity. *Ephesians: For our struggle is not against flesh and blood, but against the rulers, against the authorities, against the powers of this dark world and against the spiritual forces of evil in the heavenly realms.*

I hope that helps. I must go to sleep, he thought. However, an unsolicited thought came into his mind. *Just worship me.*

Paul kicked at the covers that had become entangled around him. Freeing himself, he came to stand in the dark. A bright light filled the bedroom, much brighter than he had ever seen. *Am I awake...or asleep?* The question pierced Paul's mind.

"Come, walk with me." Out of the light, a strong authoritative voice urged him forward. "Come," he beckoned.

Paul was dumbfounded. "What in this world is going on?" The strong voice assumed a form, but remained engulfed by the light.

"Sir, how did you get here, and where am I? This is certainly a dream even though this seems real." *But how can I make something real that is not real*, he thought, still trying to reconcile this obvious dream.

The light glared with brilliant radiance. "This is no dream. You see reality as something that you can rationalize, and in time you will redefine reality as your vision expands. There is a world around you that you are unable to define because in your reality, it does not exist. Believe me, I have seen this world, and I have been sent by our Lord to prepare you for this imminent ordeal that will threaten your reality and sanity. The Lord will require much from you."

Trying to stand while listening attentively to background sounds and attempting to peer into the light that glowed while oscillating so brightly, he asked, "Who are you?"

"We have much to see in a short time." The powerful voice paused, and then pointed past himself to a great expanse. "Look and see." There was an uncontrollable elation that overcame Paul. He could see for what appeared to be an undefined distance. There before him appeared a field with undulating hills clothed in thin knee-high green grass that swayed ever so slightly. The field was adorned with tall purple tulips. A tree line with tall green trees reached upward but never reaching a true height. They were in constant flux. No sky, but the trees had bright light piercing through them, providing ample light to see an incalculable distance through them.

A great translucent film appeared to separate Paul from the surroundings. He watched as the illuminated being passed freely between here and there. There were numerous beings, an uncountable number, that roamed freely as things appeared clearer to Paul's vision. Paul thought many were familiar, but he was not certain since they all had long left this world.

Anticipating Paul's question, the being said, "They have passed over to the land that God has given them. They live and continue in glory in a dimension void of issues. They neither reap nor sow, laugh nor cry, sleep nor rest, desire nor want, for all that they wish is at their command. A great honor they have received for their trust and obedience to the Lord, our God. This prism separates them from you while you are here." More indistinguishable images brightened beyond the prism, then faded. "These are the mansions that God has promised. Look and see."

As Paul glared across the prism, he saw his childhood friend who had died of cancer at an incredibly early age. "Gary…Gary," he called out.

"They cannot see you nor hear you because they have passed into glory. You are still in the earthly realm of the world and you may not enter. Treasure this moment and do not weep." The being of light noticed Paul's tears. "Weep for those who will never see what you have seen. Weep for the idolizers, the deceivers, and the blasphemers, and for those that curse the Holy Spirit, for their reward will be fire and brimstone. Weep for the lost and fallen, as they will never know God's love."

"Why have you shown me this, sir, Lord Angel? What are you?" inquired Paul.

"I am not your lord, but a messenger sent by God to prepare your way."

"My way?" responded Paul.

The light, still radiant, had been reduced to an immediate brightness. The expanse had disappeared, and only Paul remained with the messenger. "Take care, the darkness remains for a time still. The night is long."

"Why have you come? What is it that I am to do?" inquired Paul.

"Stay strong, for the darkness seeks your soul," admonished the light being. "Until we speak again, stay vigilant. Even as I speak, darkness closes rapidly around you and its grip seeks to break your mind and spirit, but remain steadfast because the light shall follow with great joy. Remain vigilant until we speak again." The light faded and darkness rapidly returned.

This is the craziest dream that I have ever had, Paul said, still tossing the sheets.

CHAPTER 3

One evening while in his bedroom, staring at the ceiling, following a verbal flurry of insults from his father concerning his future, Paul pondered his life's next step. Paul's eyes became fixed on the images of the Wounded Warriors Project poster mounted on his bedroom wall. There it was! He had it. He was joining the United States Army.

His parents were stunned when he informed them of his deci-sion to join the army. Had they forced him away? With war immi-nent, would they even see him alive again? Challenging Paul was his dad's way of motivating his introverted child. His dad was not trying to force him away, especially not to the military, but Paul was ada-mant; he felt giving time to his country was his responsibility. They had just forced his decision.

Answering the call of the country, Paul served faithfully for four years. It was noticeable how his confidence had exponentially grown. Gone was the timid, introverted youth who relished in his world of familiar things and fought mightily against the unknown.

Paul's decision to join the army was partially due to his social awkwardness and his preconceived ideas that adjusting to college life was going to be difficult. During his army years, he learned that attending college was actually enjoyable.

Early in his life, he had been identified by many of his teachers as gifted, and was put on a fast track to excel academically. He per-formed well in these academic endeavors, but lacked the impetus to achieve. What he actually enjoyed was reading about anything and everything.

He loved venturing into the world of make-believe, his-torical wars, the infamous dungeons and dragons, all sports and hid-den mysteries of life, why things were as they are. It totally intrigued him.

The four years that Paul served his country were rewarding and exhausting. At the end of his military tour, Paul threw in the towel and returned to the cobblestone streets of Old Town Alexandria, Virginia, again. This time as a man that knew himself better and the world—well, better than the naive kid that had departed years ago. He had done his time in the military, which he would always trea-sure. Returning home, Paul was at the crossroads again, making the decision of his career path. More confident now, it was easy.

Paul landed a job in Alexandria, working in the hospital as a laboratory technician. His tour in the army had allowed him time to receive his bachelor of science degree and subsequentially to take and pass the national laboratory exam.

Home now, Paul felt free. Free to walk the cobblestone streets, hop over the sidewalk cracks to ensure he didn't break his momma's back like he used to play with his childhood friends while growing up on West Street, as they ran from bigger boys in the narrow alleys, and jumped wooden fences between the slim-built rowhouses. That seemed like a lifetime ago.

His recollection of his early life was always prominent in his mind's eye. Recollecting how he told Daniel and his parents that he planned to enlist in the United States Army, and how they advocated against the enlistment, caused him to lament since his parents died before he returned to Alexandria this time. *Had he remained, would they have died? Who can say?* were his thoughts that seemed to always surface at odd times.v

CHAPTER 4

Rebecca Abraham was calling Daniel again, seeking a distant solace as she was being defeated by the storm. She was fully dressed and prepared to vacate her apartment at any minute. "Dear, I am totally scared, and I can't make it. This is the worst storm ever. Thunder and lightning every second, and there is no relief." She sighed deeply, fighting a tremendous urge to cry out loudly. Every light in her apart-ment was on, but still no relief from the storm.

"Go up to Paul's place and stay with him. He will not mind."

"He does not like me, he hates me," she was adamant.

"He does not hate you," replied Daniel, fighting back a yawn. "He asked about you the other day, matter of fact."

"You are just saying that because you know he hates me. He has not spoken ten words to me since Lena died, and I know he blames me for her death." Another rumble, rattling the window, sent Rebecca scrambling.

"Rebecca, not now please, I have to meet an important client early in the morning, so stay there with Paul until the storm ends. Dear, please go to Paul's and I'll call him as soon as I hang up."

"He hates me," she repeated.

"Bye, dear, I love you," Daniel ended the call abruptly. *Let me call my boy.*

Daniel had met Paul in high school math class. Daniel recalled how odd it seemed that this one black kid always appeared to separate himself from the rest of the class, and even created extra space between him and the next seated student. Daniel recollected their first conversation occurred after a fight that he had with a Palestinian student.

In his inquisitive manner—later he learned as their friendship grew—Paul approached him days later and asked why two white kids were fighting, since black and white people were historical antago-nist. He wanted to know what had caused the fight. He was about to brush him aside when he just began talking. Daniel recalled how attentive Paul was. What was hilarious was Paul's inquiry on what section of Alexandria was Palestine located.

Daniel soon learned that in Paul's world, Alexandria was either black or white, King and Duke Streets, city projects where black peo-ple were confined by race or economics. There were Chinese people, but he had no idea where they lived. Palestine had to be a section of Alexandria where white people resided, far removed from Paul's mind.

Following that meeting and against the disdainful looks from their peers, the two slowly became the best of friends and were nearly inseparable. Their friendship had been the foundation for others to emulate. Daniel knew that he could ask Paul for anything, and Paul would, to the best of his ability, try to provide whatever was requested. Even in the early morning hours, he knew Paul would help his wife, Rebecca.

Out of the door, Rebecca ran with a death grip on both her keys and cell phone. She avoided the elevator because she feared a malfunction, so she ran as rapidly as possible to the stairway and scaled the stairs to the second level. Paul's apartment was only several apartments away. She made the journey quickly.

A sudden knock on the door and the ringing on his cell phone broke his immediate dilemma. *Who in the world would be knocking or calling this late?* he wondered as a flash of lightning pierced the darkness. Paul slowly and reluctantly made his way to the door. He thought to ask who was there, but decided that his apartment com-plex was secured and security personnel controlled the entrance to the building.

"Rebecca, what are you doing out at 3:30 a.m.?" he asked. Before she could respond, he added, "And where is Daniel?" He had known the answer before asking the question. She was often jeal-ous of their friendship, which was much longer than her relationship with her husband. Ostensibly, it had caused some heated arguments that ended as quickly as they had started. Rebecca realized they were as close as brothers and her arrival could not easily separate them.

"He has flown to Chicago, on business," she said, responding to his second question. "Can I come in?" she asked.

"Certainly, come in please."

She appeared well awake and was attired in a bathrobe with colorful slippers. Her hair hung down, and she wore no makeup. "Well, thanks," she replied rather confidently. It was as if she knew that Paul would not prohibit her entrance, confident that Daniel had made the call anyway.

He wondered who had called, then looked at his cell phone, immediately recognizing the all-too-familiar name and number. Paul continued the questioning, "You know what time it is?"

"Yes, fool, and that lightning and thunder has me stone-cold scared. I am not staying in that apartment alone tonight, fool. Certainly not alone." Somehow her old charm was emerging. She was a pristine lady, a charmer to those who she was trying to impress.

"Well, I need my sleep, so you can take my room." He certainly believed that he had not gotten any sleep. "I'll give you some fresh sheets and this new comforter," he said when they got into his room, pulling the sheets and bedspread that he had been wrestling with and tossing them in the corner. Removing fresh sheets and comforter from the closet, he gave them to Rebecca. "Good night, Becky."

She hated when he called her Becky. "That's not my name, fool... Good night."

Taking a passing shot, she said, "Turn out the lights and shut that door. Daniel told me how loudly you snore."

Looking for a blanket he always had in the front room, he pulled the blanket snuggly over him. He wrapped the blanket over his head and closed his eyes. Uncertain if sleep would welcome him, he lay quietly, listening to the storm.

"Wake up, wake up," a sweet, birdlike voice called to him. A sweet silhouette danced gracefully among fields of sunflowers that playfully swayed with the light breeze. "Come to me, my love. It is I that seeks your company, so please wake up."

It cannot be, thought Paul, "Where are you?"

"I am here, look and see."

Paul wanted to run as fast as his legs would move. The silhouette seemed to keep its distance. He could not gain ground, nor would she stop. "Lena, wait! Look! It's me."

"Come to me, but you must move faster, for the wind blows me rapidly away."

The silhouette that had been fleeing slowed and fell upon the ground. The breeze slowed, and a burning heat began to make the environment uncomfortable. The sunflowers began to wither. Paul reached the figure, and it was certainly his lovely Lena.

The body rested on the ground. Her lovely eyes were closed, but her face that he had fallen so deeply in love with was radiant. Slowly, her eyes opened and began to glow a brilliant red, teeth sharpened, and a hideous smile emerged. The body morphed into a grotesque demon, and numerous demonlike companions all chuckled. Their intense disgust caused Paul to stumble backward, which exhorted them to greater joy.

"This is madness!" Paul screamed.

"Wake up, wake up," Rebecca shook Paul.

Paul awakened, flung the cover from around him, and looked around, startled. He intently stared at Rebecca.

"What is wrong with you? That teasing has caught you off guard," she spoke.

"Wow," was his only reply. Paul looked at the clock, which read 8:00 a.m., and an emerging sun cast its glow through his pulled curtains. "Isn't it time for you to leave?" he said, looking at Rebecca.

CHAPTER 5

Paul slumped in his chair, searching for the remote. Rebecca's pres-ence had engendered thoughts of his sweet Lena. Her sudden, unex-pected death had thrust him in this unabated melancholy that sur-rounded him. He had avoided his friends and associates, creating more and more excuses on why he would not be able to make what-ever they had proposed.

Even his closest friend in the world, Daniel, had not been able to offer solutions to his friend. He felt a remorse for having orches-trated the friendship that Paul and Lena shared.

Paul thought out loud, repeating a refrain that was ever present, "All things must end." He began to recall their first meeting, and it seemed to please him.

Cling, cling, ring, ring went the rhythm of the loud thunderous music that bounced off the walls of the nightclub and slithered among the countless number of dancers. The deep bass thumped and pounded repetitiously. Even the chairs appeared to be bouncing with the rhythm.

An aromatic smoke filled the room, impeded only by the solid objects that it flowed against and the small amount being absorbed.

The colorful pulsating lights brightened and darkened the room, enhancing the fun and frolicking of the people. No one com-plained, and the band played on and on, taking the delight of those inhabiting the club as encouragement.

Lena and Paul sat quietly at their booth, gazing at the crowd and searching for their friends, inwardly hoping they would be ready to go.

They had been there forever, thought Lena, and forever appeared to be how long they were going to remain. Both glanced around the room, contemplating avenues of escape.

Talking over the music was nearly impossible. When the band stopped, a DJ rapidly took their place. The music never ended, and if you came to talk with someone and watch the dancers, it was going to be a long night.

Rebecca and Daniel, soaking wet, returned to the booth to check on their friends and to see if they were having a good time. "Come on, you two," said Rebecca, tugging on Lena's hand. "You can't just sit here all night while everyone else is jamming. Dance with me," she said, again tugging Rebecca's hand, this time freeing her from the booth. "This is my song!" screamed Rebecca with renewed enthusi-asm. "Come on, girl, let's dance!"

Lena was a pitiful sight, recalled Paul, as he watched her sway one way and then another, without even any semblance of rhythm. He had met her several years ago when Lena and Daniel became friends. She also worked in the same hospital laboratory, but they infrequently spoke, and brief salutations were all she offered.

"She is a nice girl, isn't she?" asked Daniel. "No way as wild as Rebecca, is she? I knew you would like her."

"She hasn't said a word to me, and this deafening music makes talking laborious at the least," Paul replied.

"Well, you must make a concerted effort, my friend, because you don't know this, but she genuinely likes you. Your awkward ret-icence could cost you greatly," Daniel said, wiping away perspiration from his forehead. "Lena told me that she really digs you."

"Right," replied Paul.

"Well, I'm back to the dance floor, and I see my baby eyeing me now. I'll send Lena back after I tell her how much you like her." Jolting from his seat, Daniel headed straight toward his two female friends.

Paul was too slow. He could not grab Daniel. His eyes followed him to the two ladies and observed Daniel whispering in Lena's ear.

That idiot, thought Daniel. *A true idiot.*

As the evening passed, Lena and Paul sat quietly, reconciling that any conversation between the two of them would not come to fruition. They smiled when they looked at each other, and both appeared emboldened by the thought that their friend assured them the other had feelings for the other. Who was supposed to initiate this conversation? The band ended, and the disc jockey did not immediately continue to play songs.

Before Daniel and Rebecca made their way to the booth where their friends had remained, Paul quickly asked Lena, "Would you like to have lunch tomorrow at Bon Appetite?"

"Certainly, I would love to," she replied.

Paul slipped into a peaceful sleep dreaming of any variety of things. There were no terror monsters, no valley of horrors, just bliss-ful sleep. And as dreams replaced other dreams, a very bright light illuminated his surroundings.

A familiar voice spoke, "Paul, it is I. God has selected you for a great mission and many will seek to prevent your task. They will tor-ment you; they will attempt to kill you; they will cause great doubt, but you must remain resolute. The enemy of the heavens does not want the fulfilment of God's holy plan."

"Who am I?" Paul hesitated. "I am not even a great Christian." Appearing to move the light, the angel flickered, then spoke, "You were chosen many years ago, chosen by the Highest to carry out a great mission. He is omnipresent and he sees us now. He sees us always. The time of the Gentiles has ended, as written in the Book of Revelations in the Holy Bible."

"Sir, I am not a great Christian. Why would God select me for anything?" Paul was wondering if he was still asleep.

"You are asleep, but fully conscious. You will recall everything that is being spoken to you. Your soul will bear the truth of this con-versation. We will communicate this way until you can fully under-stand and believe."

"Understand and believe what?" Paul questioned.

"That the Lord God is the Living God of the Bible," answered the angel. "The devil and his minions shall seek to destroy you in an attempt to alter God's plan. I will be your protector against the darkness. Your mind will constantly and continuously confront the wiles of the darkness. They will lie, and you should not engage them. They will send people against you when you are awake and blasphemers against you when you sleep. Stay firm and call for God to assist you when you feel helpless. Your missions will range near and far. You will travel in a mist when you are given missions. I shall bring you your missions. I will always be at your side."

"I am not very well versed in the Bible. I have read and heard people quote passages verbatim." He continued, "Certainly, they will discuss or challenge me on all things biblical. What is dispensa-tionalism, or why are Christian churches so splintered? Who are the Mormons and the Jehovah's Witnesses? Are they Christians?" Paul knew his obvious shortcomings and that the church leaders would not listen to him.

"Just deliver the message. You are not being sent to defend the Word, but to make those who speak the words of God cognizant that the Lord finds them wanting. He is offering them redemption, that they might live."

The light moved and assumed a more angelic form. He reached out and waved his arms, and a great white cloud appeared before him. "This will be your vehicle. It will carry you to your destinations. Come, chosen of God; desire any place to travel and enter the cloud."

Hesitating, but moving, Paul slipped into the cloud and immediately stepped out onto the cobblestone streets of Nuremberg, Germany. The Bohnhoff was there, as were the towers that appeared to his right. The damp, misty streets and cool weather were reminis-cent of the days when he traveled these streets regularly. He loved the city, its history, and the people.

"Now step back into the cloud," urged the angel, casting his arms again.

As Paul entered the cloud, he immediately returned to his room. *What wonders,* he thought, emerging from the cloud.

Looking around the room that he was so familiar with, he noticed that time had remained the same.

CHAPTER 6

"Hey, kid," the all-too-familiar voice announced himself.

"Are you back from Chicago, dude?" responded Paul, elated that his friend called. "You have to do something with that wife of yours, and you can believe I am not going to let her in next time," he stated jokingly.

"She is in the bedroom deep sleeping now, and I thought I would give you a call. I hope she was not a big bother last night."

"No, just same old Rebecca," replied Paul. "There is something else that I want to discuss. I know you are going to call me crazy, but I need to talk to you…" He hesitated. "As soon as possible."

Daniel had known Paul all his life, it seemed. "Listen, I will leave Rebecca a note and I will be right there." Paul had appeared too serious and had eagerness in his voice.

"See you soon," replied Paul.

CHAPTER 7

Satan, the Great Deceiver, gazed over his countless minions, some crying in agony while others enjoyed the job of ensuring that those in agony remained that way. His domination was growing and growing for there were legions of lost souls that doubted the Word and many more that assumed they understood the way to God but fell far short. He believed his reign was eternal.

Satan summoned the Tormentor, Al Lost, to his side as his eyes flowed and swirled. Images danced like flowing water rippling down a creek. He transformed before the Tormentor into a great beast and roared loudly, alerting his followers that he was in their presence and that his work of snatching souls from men was his greatest desire.

He beckoned several small minions to his side and cast them into the fire. Their armor had been removed, and now they felt the torment of men. Hundreds scurried from his presence, but they knew their existence remained in peril in the Deceiver's surroundings.

"How does our work on Paul go?" the Deceiver asked his prin-cipal general. "How is his resolve?" Not waiting for an answer, he continued, "This work must be done, and quickly. We must halt God's plan before man reclaims his love of the Holy One."

"My lord," replied the Tormentor, "even now we are tormenting his teachers, probing their desires and enhancing them. Very soon the very elect will be deceived."

"Do not fail me, as you know the perils of the eternal torment. I asked about Paul, and why do you evade me? Respond truly!"

"My lord, a great angel guards him." The Tormentor stepped back. "If I may?" he asked, trying to avoid a severe physical rebuttal. The Tormentor recalled he had suffered dearly for failing in the past and was on the verge of joining men in the great pit of souls. "No mistakes, my lord, my plan—"

"I do not listen to plans," spoke the Deceiver. "Get the task done."

"Yes, my noble one," replied the Tormentor, while bowing lowly. The Deceiver had departed his presence, and to that the Tormentor was glad. His high standings in hell exalted him, and he did not want to lose that. "I will not falter in my task, Most High One."

"For your sake, see that you don't!" a voice from nowhere and everywhere in the depths of hell divisively threatened him.

More and more lost souls cried out for help, but only felt the agony of the Tormentor. "No peace for me…torment for them," he snickered.

CHAPTER 8

It was the beginning of a bright, warm spring day when Lena Elaine met Rebecca Vernon at their middle school spring festival. The festi-val was an annual event at school highlighted by students frolicking and playing games, along with plays, singing, and snacks the entire day. Although the graduating class sponsored the event, it was mainly the female students who arranged and orchestrated the venue, super-vised closely by their teachers.

It seemed only natural that the polar opposite personalities of Lena and Rebecca would find compatibility with each other. Lena, a withdrawn, very timid person who avoided the spotlight, would somehow attract the attention of the more gregarious, loud Rebecca, who loved life and living it fully.

"Hi, my name is Rebecca," she stated. She extended her hand. A broad bright smile flashed.

With her eyes looking downward, Lena exchanged the hand-shake. "My name is Lena Elaine."

For years that followed, they were never away from each other for any extended period. They attended college together, majored in the same subject, and roomed together after graduation. Even after Rebecca met Daniel and developed a close intimate relationship, they were never far apart.

Even Lena's close association with her extroverted friend could not unbridle her inner demons. She was alone in the world, embraced by insecurities and fear. She was a lovely girl. Her beautiful ebony skin punctuated by clear green eyes cast a certain mystique; however, she lived a very mundane life. She was typically attired in long dull dresses with brown loafers; her hair was black and hung down to her shoulders. She wore no makeup and rarely put on lipstick. Rebecca had, for years, tried vainly to alter Lena's personal appearance but ultimately decided to forego changing her. She was just going to be plain ole Lena.

Their relationship was very close, sincere, and lifelong. Having understood the intricacies of Lena, Rebecca never was assuming with her and always sought her agreement before deciding to include her in endeavors with others. Rebecca, the popular one, never assumed Lena would willingly socialize with others. Their friendship would forever remain unchallenged.

Later, when Rebecca prepared for her wedding, she asked Lena if being her maid of honor would cause her any concerns. When she agreed without obvious rebuttals, it was done. She knew Lena would never disappoint her, even if it was a challenge for her. She would not view her denial as a disappointment either. She loved her dearly.

CHAPTER 9

A cool wind blew briskly, soothing the multitude of people that walked in the streets. Winter had ended, and with it passing, the ensuing warmer weather was greatly welcomed. A season ended and another began.

Lena stepped from the city bus and made her way the short distance toward Bon Appetite, a stylish popular restaurant that catered to the noon-working crowd. It had been renovated recently and had quickly become the most popular dining establishment in the area.

As Lena walked, a diabolical voice interrupted her walk. *He is just tormenting you. You are so very strange. How can anyone ever love you? An evil giggle permeated her thoughts. Look at you…strange-look-ing and so very weird. How can anyone look at you without being totally disgusted? You are a total joke!* The torment continued incessantly.

Lena stopped and sought to return to the bus stop. *The voices are correct. Who, but Rebecca, ever gave me a second thought?* She was about to make an about-face when a familiar voice called her name.

"Lena, Lena, I am sorry that I am a bit late. Please don't leave." Lena turned and saw that it was Paul. "You know how the work is at the hospital," he said.

"Certainly, I am waiting for you," she replied. "You know this is my day off from work. Where else do I have to go?" She was so extremely excited and forced the evil suggestions out of her sensi-tive mind. Often wanting to speak to Paul, she was held at bay by her reticence. His refusal to accept her would be another failure, an embarrassment.

The introverted Paul gave her a warm, sincere hug. She had offered her hand, but he forced himself past it. He was cognizant of her issues, but even being introverted himself would not deter his feelings for her. She was not forceful and certainly never displayed any hidden agendas. What you saw with her was who she was.

"Let's have lunch," he said.

She smiled. "Let's eat."

Lunch was enjoyable, and she thoroughly appeared to enjoy the lunch so much so that she initiated some of the conversation. She looked and felt good. She was truly enamored with her date. *Yes, date.*

Paul's lunchtime passed so quickly, causing him to apologize to Lena for having to leave so soon. Otherwise, he would feel the wrath of his colleagues whose time for lunch would be shortened.

Lena walked home, foregoing the bus, and passed the time away with Paul occupying her mind. She would speak with Rebecca, who certainly would grill her on the day's events.

CHAPTER 10

Mary Louise Lee fumbled with the door keys to her luxurious apartment in Southeast Washington, DC. It had been a gift from her parents who sought out a safe place for their daughter, who wanted and now had a job in the workforce. She had attended a most prestigious school and graduated summa cum laude. Her parents had wanted her to remain in Savannah, Georgia, but she had a strong desire to venture out to see how others lived.

She had read extensively about other cities and sought a place where she could reside outside of Georgia. She longed for the free-dom of being away from her parents' all-seeing eyes. She attempted to appease them by moving into the apartment. They had researched the area and residence and found it acceptable.

Quickly scanning the area, she rapidly descended the red stone stairs, holding lightly to the black iron rails for support. Well-educated in the graces of being a lady, she walked, always spoke, and presented herself as a pristine lady, groomed formally in the old tra-ditions of Southern aristocracy. Even her freedom provided no relief from her upbringing, always polite and presentable.

Her father, a Southern pastor, was well respected and liked by the socialites. He had no worries or wants. His requests were tabled and handled immediately as the city's payment for him preaching the Word of God, and ensuring them that if they followed the Lord's guidance, they would once again be together in the afterlife.

Mary Louise never had an occasion, nor had she sought opportunities, to understand the ways of others outside of her limited social interactions. She was taught that a person's situation had been mapped for them at birth.

Washington, DC, habitants were prime examples of people that her parents admonished her to avoid. Well, at least the people she viewed on the news. Uneducated, quarrelsome folks who sought dis-cord and reveled in controversy.

As if she had conjured up an inner demon, Mary Louise noticed two black youths approaching her, talking very loudly and laughing wholeheartedly. She was absorbed by an imminent dilemma, causing her to breathe rapidly and shallow. Her face flushed. *Should I retreat to my apartment or proceed diagonally across the street?* Her mind and feet were not in accord; a bit of trepidation weaved a cloud of inde-cision in her mind. As the two youths approached, joking casually, pushing and tugging, their demeanor calmed as they neared Mary Louise. In her excitement, something fell from her hand.

"Ma'am, you dropped something," one of the kids said as he handed the fallen object toward her. "Ma'am, here you are."

"Ah." Nervously reaching to receive the item, timidly, she responded, "Thank you."

"Have a good day." The two kids proceeded on, momentarily without conversation, but soon lapsing back into their jovial trek.

The Uber car arrived, an older model Nissan Altima. She entered the vehicle and received a welcome smile from the driver. "To Walter Reed Hospital we go," he said.

She had not wanted to make the trip, but a longtime friend's daughter was dying. She wondered why she had told him that she would meet him at the hospital. The car smelled of incense as if it had been recently burned. The driver was listening to some elec-tronic device, his head bobbed along as he drove.

James Monroe's daughter, Charlotte, had suffered a long tedious fight with leukemia, and now the battle was ending. Mary Louise wanted to give the family her condolences and support.

The trip to the hospital went without incident. She and the driver did not engage in conversation as she sat quietly in the back seat. She was thinking a conversation might have drawn her thoughts away from the meeting that she wished to delay.

Departing the Uber vehicle, Mary Louise walked slowly to the reception desk manned by a soldier wearing military attire. Their eyes met, and a big smile adorned his face.

"Ma'am, may I help you?"

"Yes, I need to find out where Charlotte Monroe is staying," she said.

The soldier rumbled through the computer, searching the many records, until he found a record bearing the name. "Ma'am, what is her dad's name?" he said, hoping not to provide information to an unknown inquirer.

"James Monroe. Captain James Monroe."

"Thank you. She is in room 545 in the East Wing. Take the escalator to the second floor. The elevators will be to your front."

"Thank you, sir." She smiled and headed toward the escalator.

There were numerous people milling around the floors, some with directions and others seemingly just passing by. Some wore mili-tary uniforms and appeared to be attendees there, while others in mil-itary uniforms appeared to be arriving for scheduled appointments.

Mary Louise's walk toward room 545 was slow and painful. There would be nothing to cheer about and no deep-felt greetings. It was certainly an event that she was drawn toward without any desire.

As she entered the room, her eyes met the reddened eyes of her friend. The subtle sounds of sobbing were lingering. The Monroe family was hurting, deeply hurting. An end dawned in their lives, and it was imminent.

Charlotte spoke in a whisper, "Do not weep for me. I am at peace with my Lord. Cry for those that do not know God and are destined for infamy. I love you all." She died.

The angel held her hand and journeyed with Charlotte. She stopped and looked back at her family crying openly. She saw her parents crying and her brother and sister weeping. The angel smiled and led her on.

Charlotte entered a bright, pleasant setting with birds flying and singing, children running and playing, and older people engaged in conversation. Two elderly people approached her with their arms opened wide. She recognized them as her grandparents.

"Welcome, sweet Charlotte, we have been awaiting your arrival." She ran toward them with open arms. "Grandpa. Grandma," she called.

It was by far a very emotional meeting for Mary Louise with her friend's family. There was no way she thought that she could ever share the feelings that the Monroe family was feeling. No words would be sufficient to ease their loss. Her presence was all she could give.

Mary rode home in a taxi after departing the hospital, still tired from the mental anguish that tormented her following the death of young Charlotte.

Death and life were juxtaposition, but the loss of friends never made it easy. *If there, in fact, is an afterlife, she thought, I hope that I meet my lost friends again.* She wept in silence, attempting to avoid the taxi driver's wandering eyes.

CHAPTER 11

Paul, Daniel, and Rebecca sat in the hospital cafeteria, eating lunch. They sat among the diners with a multitude of sounds and smells. It was for the most part a jovial atmosphere with colleagues and friends engaging in a variety of conversations, mostly centered on their work or teasing each other.

Unless you were in the immediate vicinity, you would not be able to discern the crux of any conversation. Since Paul, Daniel, and Rebecca were personal friends, they were more relaxed and chose to find humor in Rebecca's escapades during the most recent storm. Their laughter was calculated and defined. When they were together, no formalities existed. Rebecca loved laughing, as it helped with the lingering effects of her lost friend, Lena.

Paul recognized that much of the focus had been cast on him and accepted it in good humor. Daniel had suggested the gathering so they could relieve feelings as they had often done so many times before. "Here comes Mary Louise," announced Rebecca.

Mary Louise approached the table with her charming smile and a small purse held solidly in her hand. She was obviously different from the people in the cafeteria and wore a degree of aristocracy, whether consciously or implied. Daniel rose and helped her with her seat, which caused Paul to make an inquiring eye contact with his friend.

Rebecca introduced Mary to Paul. She did not linger on the introduction and immediately engaged her on her recent promotion within the hospital. Rebecca being normally scheming, there was no subtle intentions in her introduction. This was not the time or place to engage in her life's passion of matchmaking. She had recently lost the dearest friend she ever had, and in her mind, she believed Paul felt the same.

They continued their conversation, lacking the robust needling that was ever-present when they were together as a threesome. Mary would have to grow on them a while until she would be privy to their personal secrets.

CHAPTER 12

It was not a trip that Lena wanted to make, but a concession. She acquiesced to avoid unpleasantries, and she loved this man, so her decision to accompany him was bittersweet. She did not want to go, but she enjoyed dearly their association. She had become a pawn of the night. A fading sunset, the darkness of the evening opened her eyes, and it sheltered and shielded her.

Lena and Paul walked down King Street, playfully poking each other and looking in each store window, suggesting that they pur-chase an abstract picture, rug, or figurine to decorate Paul's mundane apartment, which was replete with pasted pictures of the Beatles, Hendrix, and Bob Marley, along with a picture of Roberto Clemente. She was going to add life to this apartment.

Lena leaned on her friend, Rebecca, much of her short life, and only her friend. However, now, Paul had become a loving substitute, and her feelings for him equaled the love she had only shared with Rebecca. They seemed to always be together now. She found a dif-ferent pleasure with Paul, a warm inner feeling that caused her blood to rise. Her hesitation with others fell away; Lena felt born anew. A brisk breeze rushed them but had no effect on their playful exchange.

Lena's mood abruptly turned as she noticed a small child seem-ingly transfixed by her. The child held in a tenuous gaze seemed impaled by the ebony-skinned lady with clear crystal green eyes. It was a reoccurring situation with her particularly with the young. It would trigger flashbacks to an earlier period in her life when she was tormented by so-called friends and classmates.

"Let's go home, Paul. I'm tired," she suggested.

"We haven't looked in all of the windows, my dear Lena," Paul answered. He reached for her hand, but she withdrew from him.

"What went wrong, dearest?" he asked.

"I just want to go home."

This was not so unfamiliar with Lena, who tolerated being outside rather than wanting to go to any particular place. She could never reconcile being teased or being some aberration that caused others to stare. Paul tried to recreate a new world for her, but always felt that she was two people. One with him and one that feared jour-neying out. He thought that she was always in constant turmoil with no solutions.

They returned to the apartment complex in total silence. Lena looked toward Paul and offered a half smile that was void of feeling. She fought inner demons that mentally tormented her often. Life was miserable for her, and even her colleagues were uncomfortable around her. She did not understand them, and they understood her less.

Lena kissed Paul on the cheek and spoke, "I'll talk with you later. I just need some rest."

"Do you want some company?" he asked.

She held him close and smiled. "You have always been my company ever since we met. In truth, I have never loved anyone, except Rebecca, more than I love you." She bowed her head and repeated, "Never." Her eyes met his, but she turned away.

He realized that she was adamant and wanted to remain alone. Grasping her hand, he pulled her to him and hugged her tightly. "I'll see you soon," he said.

Lena walked toward her apartment, and Paul looked at her and headed for his. *She needs a little more time. I'll see her later,* Paul thought.

CHAPTER 13

Mount Zion Baptist Church was an exceptionally large church with an attendance that exceeded one thousand and whose membership was three times greater. A universally renowned place of worship that welcomed hundreds from around the world yearly. It gave Baltimore, Maryland, a good reputation that every visitor, regardless of ethnic-ity, race, or gender, had a place to visit and worship. Many received their baptisms there regardless if they were members or not. God must surely have blessed this sanctuary and pastor.

It was adorned with detailed stained glass. There was a hun-dred-seat choir set behind the pastor's pew, which rested on a lavish raised floor that gave him an advantageous and favorable position above his flock. The pews were cushioned and extremely comfort-able. A ten-foot gold replica of Jesus hung prominently displayed above the congregation. It was a modern splendor, a powerful ren-dition that echoed the sentiments of an enslaved rooted people that had long ago been baptized in the blood of Jesus. God found it want-ing and was not pleased.

"Amen! Thank you, Jesus! Sing!" rose from the assembled mass, and the cries rang loud and long. The pastor, as on cue, rose and slowly made his way to the pulpit. He did not wait to be announced, but jumped into the worship, reaping continuous praise from his flock.

The choir had just finished singing "What a Friend We Have in Jesus".

With the arrival of pastor at the podium, an electric atmosphere flushed the congregation with emotions that neared hysteria. People

35

shouted "Hallelujah! Hallelujah!" reaching a crescendo that echoed throughout.

Roy Lee Johnson joined in exhorting the congregation to greater heights. "Hallelujah!" he jubilantly urged the crowd on. "What a great day to be in the House of the Lord."

The music, led by the church band, encouraged the attendees to greater ecstasy as they abandoned their seats and danced rhyth-mically to the sounds that rang freely, bordering on unsanctified worldly music.

The pastor joined in on the emotionally charged atmosphere by prancing around. He had been caught up in the emotions of his congregation. "Take me, Lord, I want to go home!" he called. He yelled and yelled.

Some people fell upon the floor and began to speak in strange languages as many more joined in. People wept and shouted. The time was about right.

Pastor Johnson raised his hands, but the shouting and applause did not fade. Echoes of "amen" slowly faded. For the parishioners, it was heartfelt. They voiced their desires, and this was a time that they were free, free to be with their God.

As the shouting ceased, the pastor began, "My brother and sister, fellow servants of the highest, my God Jesus Christ, I have heard from God, and he wants you to live and live forever." He slowly walked over to the church's prophet. He wiped his brow as drips of sweat escaped with the swipe. "Prophet Leon Hill, what does God want us to do?"

Prophet Hill slowly stood. His black lens shielded his brown eyes. The lens had given him a mystic appearance. "I have listened to the cries of the people, and the Lord has whispered in my ear. The Lord has whispered in my ears! Pastor, they don't hear me!" Shouts erupted, exhorting him further. He raised his hands, quieting the believers.

"Listen closely," admonished Pastor Johnson, as a black smoke raised and swirled from a light artificial breeze. "Hear what God has asked me to deliver. Hear me, my brothers and sisters."

Pastor Johnson, seemingly propelled by an unknown force, backed away. His eyes appeared to be transfixed on Prophet Hill. The members in the church paid a greater attention to the pulpit.

Paul emerged outside of the church. There were numerous vehicles parked in this large parking lot, even the overflow lot was filled. He thought this lot appeared to have any number of luxury vehicles. "I should jump in one and drive off." He giggled. He was on another assignment. This time to bring the message to Pastor Johnson that the Lord God was not pleased with his antics and that his time as pastor had ended.

Suddenly, a familiar voice spoke to Paul's conscious mind. *There is a family that is approaching the church. Speak with them and admonish them not to attend church today. Tell them that I will speak to them in mind and thoughts in a time and prepare them for the journey they will take.*

"Suppose they don't listen to me, and enter the church?" Paul asked.

Why do you continue to doubt the will of God? His sheep know him, and he knows his sheep. Remember you are never alone. Get about God's work.

A man, his spouse, and two small children approached the church. They were well attired, dressed in their Sunday's best. The kids smiled and danced along while the father led them toward the church door. He held a worn leather Bible in his hand and his spouse's hand in the other.

Approaching the family, Paul greeted them. "Good morning, sir... ma'am. How are you?" Paul fumbled with the greeting and did not know why he was restless.

"Well...and you, sir?" the tall slender man replied. He momentarily stopped.

"What I am about to say is going to sound crazy, but God does not want you to enter this church. His judgement is on it," Paul managed to say.

The man looked at Paul, and simply smiled.

"You know, something in my soul was steering me away from here today. But..." He paused. "I had heard such wonderful reviews about the pastor and the church. I spoke with one of the deacons, and he was cognizant that we were looking for a church and sug-gested that I come here."

Paul replied while shifting his stance, "I have never been inside." The gentleman then introduced himself as Fred. He introduced his spouse and children. For some reason, he was quite comfortable with Paul.

"I guess we will try another church in the area." Before depart-ing, he asked Paul, "Where do you attend church?"

"I am not from here, sir, just here to complete an assignment," he answered. "Take care, sir. I hope you find a good holy church." He winked at the kids, who were looking at him.

Paul entered the prestigious building. Its ornate windows were marvelous, and the rows of walnut-made benches with cushioned seats added amenities not always seen. The ushers hurriedly directed him to an available seat as they attentively watched the prophet and the pastor.

God had sent Paul to speak to the pastor, the first lady, and the prophet concerning their false representation, and to inform them that God wanted them to return all their possessions to the church. Because their acts were so blatant and egregious against the Lord, their fall should be equally embarrassing.

Paul felt this situation could have been resolved outside of the church, but was rebutted harshly by the angel, who informed him that his job was to fulfill his assignment without question.

The so-called prophet began to speak incoherently as dark bil-lowing smoke began to engulf him. The churchgoers looked on in wonderment. They were mesmerized by the so-called prophet, who hinted he certainly was misunderstood by the congregation.

Inside the church, Paul could hear Prophet Hill saying, "Search your souls. Today I convey a truth given directly to me by God." The congregation did not utter a sound, and only infants' unsettled movements broke the silence.

"This appointed pastor, our Pastor Johnson, has pleased the Lord God, and as such, there should be a special offering collected and given to him and his family for God's work. A work that he is unable to speak of due to God's admonishment. This work could have been bestowed on many others, but the Lord has found special favor in our pastor. Henceforth, he shall be called Bishop Johnson. So search your pockets, wallets, and purses, and when the plate is passed, do not hesitate to provide what you can give. God will not forget your sacrifices this day."

Unaware of this special offering, the ushers proceeded to their respective collection areas around the church. Veteran ushers occu-pied these positions, and they were versatile and responded quickly to the church's business.

During the collection process, an old gospel melody played in the background as the choir instantly launched into a song.

The newly appointed bishop's wife attired in a firm, skin-clutch-ing dress partially covering her breasts, brought a drink and a hand-kerchief to wipe the bishop's forehead.

The unholy minions gathered. There were many and appeared to flourish in this fallen church. They appeared as dark shadows cir-cling the church. They urged the parishioners to empty their wallets to honor a holy prophet in their midst. They could only suggest, but were well received.

The larger and more hideous servants of hell surrounded the pulpit, occasionally enhancing the bishop's and the false prophet's visions of grandeur.

Paul was aware that he would not be well received and felt panic and anxiety stack in his mind. He grasped his head with sweaty hands as he tried to gain the courage to confront the pastor. Although hesi-tant, he felt the power of the Holy Spirit urging him forward.

No one appeared to notice Paul as he slowly made his way for-ward. He passed many rows of jubilant parishioners, seeming encour-aged by the announcement.

Standing immediately near the pulpit, a dark challenge con-fronted him. It was overwhelming and sent Paul's unprepared mind into a manic episode, forcing him backward.

Stand firm against evil principalities and dark forces. Put on your armor, an encouraging voice whispered to his mind. *They have no control over you. But be vigilant, they want you for their own.*

Bishop Johnson approached the front of the pulpit, his wife slowly following. "How can I help you?" His face contorted with anger toward Paul.

Paul, reeling from the spiritual attack, stood directly in front of the church leadership, who were now joined by other ministers in the pulpit. He wondered why they were confronting him because he had not delivered any message. However, now emboldened, he spoke, "The Lord God has sent me to you," his voice excited. "Abdicate your position and turn it over to the deacon board. Your antics and messages have insulted God, and his people now stand tentatively on the cliff while the devil gathers the souls of those that do not believe."

Prophet Hill interceded, "This is Bishop Johnson, a holy man ordained and anointed by God's word."

"This is a child of the Great Liar, along with you and others here in the pulpit." The podium suddenly vaulted forward, falling toward Paul, who easily evaded it.

Bishop Johnson instructed Deacon Randall to call the police. He immediately pulled his cell phone from his suit jacket's inner pocket and attempted to dial 911, but cell phones were not receiving a signal.

The congregation now began to wonder what the commotion was about. Their attention became directed toward the pulpit.

The assault on Paul's mind nearly felled him, but he stood and staggered. He had never faced the mental fury of evil that rattled his brain. Evil had a tenacious hold on the hierarchy of the church and would not relinquish it easily. This interloper was attempting to unravel a well-planted seed that would bear countless fruit.

A soothing voice began to encourage him, *I shall fear no evil; for thou art with me; thy rod and thy staff they comfort me.* With renewed vigor, Paul asked the newly appointed bishop to gather his governing body and leave the church, abdicate his position publicly, and ask God for forgiveness.

An imp whispered to Bishop Johnson, "There is no God, only a child's story to keep people doped so they can tolerate their miserable lives. You are their god. They adore you and worship you."

Bishop Johnson called out, "I am God here on earth, your savior!" The congregation sat frozen in their seats. He had planned to make this announcement later, but being forced into this position by the events of the past few moments, he had to announce it now.

Several men clad in combat attire burst through the church doors, screaming and yelling blasphemies and racial epithets. Their hands held automatic weapons that began to speak loudly. Thousands of bullets sprayed the church. Paul felt he was being pulled to the ground and fell abruptly to the floor. Nameless bullets riddled the church, and several passed over him. The bullets had a mission, and they aimed to complete it.

Evil had turned on evil, and the entire raised area where the bishop and his command stood were riddled with automatic weap-ons fire. Their bodies convulsed and fell hard to the floor.

The shooters departed as rapidly as they had come after spread-ing their terror. They continued to yell and holler obscenities while fleeing like the cowards that they were. Unholy minions tore into each other. The new arrivals had interfered with the enormous num-ber of souls they would have secured for their demon god. He had been pleased with their efforts and stood in their presence, but now they were suffering profoundly, and it was not their fault. Evil had taken its toll on unexpecting souls.

People ran in all directions, some hiding on the floor while others sought out the exits that were cluttered with bodies, attempting to flee the scene of terror. Babies screamed, and the entire place was a calamity.

No one in the pulpit survived the assault. Bishop, prophet, and deacon were felled by bullets to the head while Johnson's wife choked on blood from a wound to her lungs. Some people ran to the pulpit, but most milled around, overcome by fright.

Paul stood and stepped into the cloud, arriving home to the sound of children's laughter on West Street. He sat on his favorite chair and wept loudly as the recent events that surrounded him were so vivid. The angel stood beside him and called his name, Paul.

"I do not want to do this anymore. I'll take my chances during the judgment." Paul was distraught and mentally disturbed.

Why do these senseless events challenge your faith? God has given you a profound favor. He has bestowed his grace on you. Yet, you still ponder events that have been secreted from the world for centuries and now manifest themselves. Others would jump for joy to know that God has favored them. The angel paused, then continued, Those that have little faith would willingly take on this mission, yet you question every little thing.

Shuffling in his seat and wanting to speak, Paul was harshly silenced by the light. *One day when you are at rest in the many mansions, you will ponder your actions and wonder why God did not dismiss you and allow the evil one to cast you into the fire of the faithless. Prepare yourself, you have work to do…such a pitiful sight. When faced with evil, you trembled even when I assured you that nothing would happen to you. What has been written will be done. Get up!* he ordered. *Time is running short.* The light faded, leaving Paul in a worse mental mess. He would never doubt the Living God again. At least not today.

Fred Maynard and his spouse, Jiri, along with their children, gathered in the living room. They stood in a circle sealed with the clasping of their hands and bowed their heads in reverence. Fred began to pray, "The highest God, my God, Jesus Christ, I have no explanation or why you intervened today. My family is safe and our love for you is great. For whatever reason you spared us today from the atrocious activity that felled members of that holy church, I am deeply indebted. We shall always serve you and keep you first in our lives. Ask me whatever you need of me and it shall be done. In the name of my Holy God, Jesus Christ, we pray."

A voice spoke to him, spoke to his mind as if the person was standing next to him. After opening his eyes, he looked sideways toward where the voice emerged. The voice whispered again, *Dark forces shall seek you out. Stay firm in your belief. I shall send a message to you, and it will be delivered by another of God's servants. Heed his words and follow them explicitly.* The voice fell silent.

Fred wondered if his wife heard anything, or was this a conversation in his mind? *These are strange days indeed,* he thought.

CHAPTER 14

The western part of Virginia had recently been covered by an unexpected late-season snowfall. The road clearing apparatus had prematurely slipped into its summer protocol and was a bit embarrassed by efforts to clear the snow from the covered landscape. It was, however, a breathtaking sight as the snow and the greenery of spring provided an eloquent contrast.

Stewart, a very small city with a single road, was entirely cov-ered by seven inches of snow. The city sat juxtaposed an extended mountain range base.

The road gradually began an extended climb high into the mountain range, and after a gradual descent, came close to pass-ing into West Virginia. Green vegetation filled with various tree types, wildflowers, and wandering vines created a picturesque view. However, today the snow impeded movement along the road by vehicle travel.

Pastor Grant Longstreet had a rendezvous with the congrega-tion of his church this beautiful Sunday morning as he viewed it. He had over fifty years of being the pastor at this small Southern church, and in the time that he had been pastor, he never missed a service. He would always honor God by teaching the Word, and short of death, he would always be in the pulpit.

This morning, his walk to the church, which would be about two miles from his home and pass directly through town, would be slightly hindered by the weather. He had always arrived at the small community church early to adjust the furnace to make the arrival of the flock as comfortable as possible. Dressed for the unexpected weather, Pastor Longstreet headed for work…God's work.

Very few people were about, and cars slowly traveled the main street, which had succumbed to the snow. Everyone that saw Pastor Longstreet asked if he needed a ride, but he politely refused. Some people circled the block. They loved this elderly pastor and wanted to be near him should he need assistance.

The local sheriff, John Pickney, who happened upon the pas-tor on his way to church, drove up. "Pastor Longstreet, get out of this weather. You will catch a terrible cold out here in this dreadful weather. Get in, let me do something useful this morning."

"John, thanks, but I need this time to commune with Jesus." He smiled.

"I can get you to church in minutes, and you'll have some free time."

"Thanks again, but this elderly body needs some exercise some-times, and this little journey will certainly provide that."

"Okay, but I'll be there for service, and on time. Maybe some-one will need assistance."

"Be safe, John, and I'll see you later."

John drove off, driving around the corner and watching the pas-tor make his journey. If the old man needed assistance, he would be there.

Pastor Longstreet walked slowly across the fresh snow, taking caution not to become a victim of the ice. The sun was slowly rising, which allowed a greater distance to view. There was snow everywhere. As he negotiated the snow, he peered occasionally into store windows that were closed and would not open until Monday. There appeared to be shadows circling the pastor as he traversed the short distance.

Grant wondered from whence these objects had come. He looked toward the sun and searched for objects casting shadows, but without answers. Even the snow became more difficult to walk and the soft snow had changed to a sheet of ice. The pastor was about to turn the corner when a soft-spoken lady called to him. Astonished because of the familiarity of the voice, he turned to speak to the per-son behind the voice. He faced an elderly lady.

"Why are you here in this inclement weather at this hour? It will soon be much better because the residents will clear pathways for their neighbors. Can I help you?" he said warmly.

"Oh, I am fine. The weather is lovely this time of year, and I just wanted to enjoy it," she responded. "I just left South Goering just a while ago. Such a despicable place," she said.

"I was a bit shocked when you mentioned that godless place. I am surprised that you would even go there. Do you have relatives there?" he asked.

"No, just traveling through. Its reputation preceded it. There did not appear to be any godly people there. I guess they will be judged accordingly. Such a den of iniquity."

"There is nothing open at this time." Looking around, he did not notice anyone in the vicinity, nor was he able to resolve a big question in his mind. *How and where did this lady come from?*

Subtle voices attacked him. *She is a lunatic and almost certainly lost. Pastor, you have greater things that must be done now, and dealing with her is going to make you late.*

Grant recognized that he was being demonically assaulted by Satan or his minions. He now recognized the shadows as demons, and he knew that they did not want him to slow down.

The pastor spoke clearly, "In the name of Jesus, get behind me, Satan! There is no truth in you."

The sheriff reappeared after observing the pastor had stopped and was looking around. He had driven to his current location, which was only a short distance and close to Pastor Longstreet.

John asked, "Pastor, are you well? Is everything okay? I saw you turning around and appeared to be talking to yourself."

"There was an elderly lady walking behind me. Have you seen her?"

"No, sir," he said. "I saw you turning around, and drove here. Is there something that I can assist you with? I saw no lady," he said.

A loud explosion startled both the sheriff and Pastor Longstreet. The town's only church was now on fire and burning intensely. It appeared to be burning rapidly, faster than any they had ever seen.

The pastor wanted to run to the church, but the sheriff had vacated his vehicle and held the pastor securely. He relaxed his grip as Pastor Longstreet watched years of his life fade into the morning. Grant looked around and wondered where the lady had gone. Had she delayed him long enough to keep him free from the flames? The dark shadows flew around the church in total glee, happy that they had destroyed another church.

People began to appear, and an emergency vehicle arrived to fight the flames. The flames had won this battle, and with good sin-cere efforts, which were futile, the crowd grew, and many began to cry. Their remorse was great.

Pastor Longstreet knelt along with those that had gathered with him and prayed the Lord's Prayer. Others followed his lead, and a great joy overcame them. "We will rebuild the church and no demons of hell will win this day." He prayed.

CHAPTER 15

Charles Schmidt intently read a manifest that had been written by a very hateful group. They had advocated the return of white peo-ple's control of the government. They denounced minorities, viewed homosexual living as an abomination, and blamed the death of Jesus on the Jewish people.

Charles, for unknown reasons, identified with this rhetoric. It was an enlightenment that was deep-rooted in the destiny of the white people. He was an A student and excelled in the scholarly world. Many awards decorated his walls, and he certainly would be accepted into one of Virginia's more prestigious institutions upon graduating from high school. He appeared to have a bright future.

His family was prominent citizens. They were well liked in this small community and enjoyed similar favor with the residents of Stewart as did Pastor Longstreet. The only requirement they placed on their son was that he always maximized his mental talents, which were noteworthy.

Knowledge did not seem to appease the young man as he wanted to see action. Rhetoric was only a means to an end. He sought more.

A doctor from India had accepted a position at a nearby hospital and moved into the all-white community. It had not taken long for bigoted messages to surface. Although Christian in beliefs, the small town of Stewart was more prone to accept stereotypes than truth. There were no anti-nonwhite rallies or flyers denouncing them, but hate had found root.

Initially, Dr. Raji had endured the subtle suggestions that he would probably find a much better area to practice his profession even though the city lacked a medical doctor. But slowly, with much assistance from Pastor Longstreet, his family endured and became members of the small town. The community began to relax their objections and accepted the doctor. Dr. Raji became a regular at nearly all the community events and shared traditional foods with the community.

The city was active, and they held church, social community, and many other affairs. The police supported the community, and the community supported the police. Obvious crime was never apparent here in Stewart.

But Charles saw the foreign presence as the beginning of the end for Stewart. He knew there would be few in the beginning, then the numbers would increase. Cultural confrontations were held in abeyance for now, but discord was beginning.

As Charles became enthralled with his bigotry, he contemplated methods to retaliate against the foreigners. He would first unroot the bastion of their threatened unity. He must restore tradition and attack the radical Christian beliefs that promoted love for all by establishing a new white rule and destroying the reputation of the influence of the community church. This would fuel his platform, and he felt that he could now join with the nationwide plight of the truly disconnected. He believed the white man was the creator of civilization, and he had to sustain the momentum of whites whose actions were greater than just thoughts.

He had to be seen as the champion of the cause, so action was a necessity. Charles had gathered a large gas can and filled it with gasoline. He knew what needed to be done.

With credits, he would be recognized by the united front as an activist. An inner voice encouraged him, whispering to his consciousness, *You are doing the right thing. The citizens will realize that a violent change was necessary, and your actions shall be celebrated in the near future. White people are becoming extinct, and a strong rebuttal to the decline is necessary.*

The salacious working of evil had won another victim. Another member of the forlorn, who found their reality in untruth. They subliminally urged support and offered him encouragement. *Immigrants, blacks, Jews, and the poor are uprooting our society. Listen, they don't work. They add nothing to society but vile music and make mongrels of our pure white women. Look at the bastard children! Look how they live and look how they are tearing the cities apart.*

Charles was totally overcome by his newfound cause. A new convert of hate.

He read extensively, emboldened by pride, and began to prepare for his cause. He would be celebrated. Many would champion his cause after the blame of his salacious plan would be cast only upon the foreign members of the city.

It was time now for action. He wore dark camouflage attire to allow himself to blend with the early morning darkness. Since the community was rather small, concealment was required. Everyone knew everyone else in the city. After parking on one of the forest roads, Charles vacated his vehicle and slipped into the thick rows of trees. He slipped from the forest to the rear of the community church. Since the church was never secured, Charles easily gained entrance and poured the vile liquid throughout.

The demons overwhelmed his mind and shouted great praise upon him. *Have no second thoughts. You are doing the right thing, they whispered. You will be a great man one day, and the white man will reap praises upon you.*

Demons dwelled upon those inclined to racial intolerance. They were the easy victims of distorted minds that clamored for purity. Convince the least intelligent without altering their core ideas. Filter in hateful events supported by faces of the group you attempted to dehumanize and cast their actions as inhuman, and the least edu-cated in the group will champion the cause without conscious thought. They were well-taught and preyed upon hate. Charles was just another victim. The demons regaled him.

The morning light pierced the windows, and the church brightened. Charles took out a lighter and cast it upon the floor. He rapidly sought out his escape as the fire roared. Sheer ecstasy overcame him.

The explosion and the all-consuming flames engulfed his surroundings. Finding the door at the rear of the church, he darted forward; however, he was abruptly stopped by sheer fear as a dark shadow barred his way. *Who is that, and where did it come from?* he thought. An unholy joy had satiated him, but now faded.

The flames consumed everything within the old church. Charles, hurting from his burns, now watched as the shadow took form. He shouted for his mother, but he heard only the chuckling of this new form. "Well done, faithful one," it whispered.

"Where am I?" he fearfully asked.

"Don't you know?" asked the large form. "You have been granted your wish to join forces with the Dark Lord and his minions. You are in hell," he laughed. "You have come home by your desires, and here you are."

Charles cried in pain as he felt the tormenter torching him. He wanted to run, but was bound by small minions that snacked on his soul while shouting obscenities. "You are home, your eternal home," they taunted him.

Charles ran, seeking an avenue of escape from the burning inferno, without success. As the flames roared, Charles cried out in agony, while the devil's minions laughed aloud and praised the devil. Evil had claimed another.

CHAPTER 16

A warm southerly breeze doused the people of Stewart. The snow that had apparent unknown origins now faded as rapidly as it came. The vegetation that was mostly brown softly and delicately began to change. A small hill arrayed in its natural vegetative beauty, a short distance from the historical church, became the gathering place for the inhabitants.

Pastor Longstreet spoke, "Please take a seat," raising his hands. "Sit in peace," he spoke. He gathered his black robe together and stood like a stone wall behind a lectern where some had gathered. He was always faithful and held no animosity toward whoever had burned his beloved sanctuary.

Grant had been informed that a body burned beyond recog-nition was found. He wondered who it might have been, and why would they burn the church? Could they not have escaped the inferno? Many questions assaulted him, but none had any answers. "Let us begin this service by reciting the Lord's Prayer…Our Father who art in Heaven… Amen."

"The church building has died, but not our resolve. I have received numerous telephone calls from known and anonymous sources pledging to rebuild the church as soon as they receive the okay. Give God the praise! Let us pray for the soul that has been lost in this most tragic incident. May his soul rest in peace."

Jewish leaders from nearby communities who knew Pastor Longstreet, along with Christian believers, gathered and offered regret and love for the faithful. At this time and place, there were no condemnations for anyone or anything. It was a gathering that the world would and could appreciate.

As the long day ended, the gathering of people made their way back home. Their hearts were heavy, but their hope was alive. Whatever or whoever had been the cause of this foolish act had not won this day.

Returning home, Grant eased himself into his lounge chair and felt his body exhale. He wondered why this had happened and who was responsible. Sleep overcame Grant, but he felt fully awake.

Sleep always rests a body worn by the trials of the day. This day's events had conquered the elderly man. He had given no struggle and drifted quietly into the land where dreams dwell. Subject to the fantasy of dreams, sleep played games independent of human desires.

In the world of heaven and hell, angels and demons battled for supremacy. They followed the will of their masters, whose desire was to gain souls. Good for God and evil for Satan.

Pastor Longstreet was no exception. Unknown to him, he was now a participant in the struggle between good and evil. He stirred, reflecting the uneasiness of his sleep.

"Old man, your time nears in the material world, but fear not for my master has sent me to make you a generous offer, very gen-erous. He is aware of your desire to save your brothers and sisters and wants you to continue your work." Appearing very debonair, the minion assumed human form, creating unrealities filled with human desires.

"What and who are you, sir?" asked Grant. "Where have you come from, and where am I?"

"In time, I will answer your questions, but what do you want most of all in your life?"

"Are you from God?" questioned the unconscious Grant.

"I am from the spiritual realm, a never-ending realm, and we want you to have whatever your heart desires. Look and see, Mr. Longstreet, at these souls…worn down, injuries, diseases, and phys-ical impairments, and you can help them by your presence. Their calamities will wither at your command."

Grant was taken aback. The demon felt the hesitance. Was he asleep, or was he actually here? A small youth, Charlotte, ravished with cancer, and her family alongside her hospital bed, weeping, appeared to be praying. The demon passed the situation with skillful aplomb. Grant appeared to be there in the hospital room with Charlotte at Walter Reed.

"Just walk to the bed and take her hand, and exercise your power over death, and she shall live. Just do it." The demon had become extremely excited as he felt the prey near the snare.

Grant felt an overwhelming power ease through his body. Could he command life and death? Was God giving him a special gift?

The minion urged him, "Just do it. You have the power of life and death."

A tiny pleasant voice uttered, "Do not weep for me. I am at peace with my Lord. Cry for those that do not know God and are destined for infamy. I love you all." She died.

Grant awoke and prayed. He had been in the midst of evil and desired the gift that was offered. It had been a crossroad. Although he did not totally understand what had happened, he prayed for strength from God. Spiritual warfare was ever present and he held strong to his faith.

Grant was now fully awake and noticed that the strange events from his slumber and the physical world had ended. He had remained in his old comfortable chair and had not kept his appointment with his bed. The sun had risen, clearing away the night that had tor-mented him. He attempted to recall the nightly events, but struggled with any lucid recollection. A subtle thought arose in his mind, *Fear not for God hears you.*

Let me gather breakfast, he thought as he realized he was overly famished. Toast, butter, and orange juice would be his immediate solution. After attending his morning ritual, he waited and eventu-ally gathered his breakfast. He prayed to God for his food.

Tap, tap, tap on his door slightly startled him, and again the sound repeated. "Who is up at this time and need my assistance?" Leaving his meal, he pushed back from the table, ensured he was properly dressed, and opened the door. There was an unknown black male standing there, smiling.

Without reservation, he spoke to the stranger, "How may I help you, sir?"

"Pastor Longstreet?"

"I am he."

"Pastor, I have a message for you from your Lord and Savior, Jesus Christ. I know it is different and that you may have some degree of trepidations, but believe me this is real, and I am bringing you a message from God."

"Sir, come in." He beckoned to the stranger. *So strange these events surrounding the church,* he thought. "For some reason, I have a good feeling about you. Come in, come in," he repeated. He directed the young man to a seat in the living room. "Sir, do you want any-thing to drink or eat?"

"Thank you, but no," he replied. "I only recently enjoyed a big breakfast."

Pastor Longstreet wondered to himself where such a meal came from at this early morning hour. He noticed it was about 7:30 a.m. There were no fast-food establishments in town and the restaurant did not open until after eight.

Seeing that the pastor, who was now seated, appeared to won-der, he offered, "Last evening a light being, or angel, that I am quite familiar with told me that I needed to meet with you this morning. He comes to me with various instructions from God. At first it was strange to me, but after some reticence, I simply followed the direc-tives that I had been given. My current new mission is you."

Pastor Longstreet began to recite the Lord's Prayer. He always found assurance when he gave himself freely to the will of God. *If this man was from God, he would be revealed.*

Paul did not wait for Pastor Longstreet to respond, "You shall gather the saints from around the country, starting here in Stewart, and travel until God signals the end of your journey. As you trek across the country, others will join you." Abruptly, he stopped, "That is your mission." Paul was never subtle and presented to Pastor Longstreet what was told to him.

"How am I going to get anyone to drop their lives and uproot and follow me?" He thought of the logistics of such an event. "How do I feed anyone, and what vehicles will I use?"

"You shall make this journey by faith and travel by foot. God will provide all that you will need."

Stewart was coming to life as the early morning sounds could be heard. The sound of cars and a few greetings between lifelong friends helped to announce the day's beginning.

"Sir, I am not saying that I do not believe you, but there is a degree of hesitation here. There are very influential and affluent peo-ple that call this small city home. I cannot ask them to give up their lives that are firmly planted here and journey nearly halfway across the country. I just do not feel that this is right. You cannot ask this of me."

"It is not I that asks this of you. It is as your God commands. You must be about the business of God."

"I'll have to pray on this, sir."

Paul was sure that the message that was given to him to deliver had been done. As he prepared to stand, an urge to ask Grant a ques-tion overcame him. "Pastor, when you were young, a young black kid was playing in his yard. You and your friends started to throw rocks at him. Several of the rocks struck him and he fell to the ground. You and your friends ran away laughing. You may not know this, but the kid was paralyzed and has not walked or talked since then."

Grant's face reddened, and his eyes filled with tears. He always wanted to forget that incident, and he believed God had forgiven him this indiscretion. "How are you cognizant of this incident?" he spoke, deeply saddened as he struggled to maintain his control.

Paul said, "This knowledge is from God. People rely on wonders and mysteries. He has more to provide should you need them. He wants you to get about his work."

Paul now had risen from his seat and walked toward Grant. He placed his hand upon the shoulder of the weeping man.

Grant felt a strange calmness surrounding him, and the pains of age seemed to drift away. He looked at Paul, who only smiled.

"Pastor, your work begins, so gather those who hear the Lord's words and shall follow you. Be vigilant, for when the devil becomes aware of your work, he shall travel about to devour you and those with you. Take care, for there are angels that shall guard you until your work is done. Be not afraid, our mission is waiting for you."

A tremendous cloud filled the room, causing Grant to want to run. Fear had claimed him. Paul turned and smiled, and stepped into the cloud.

The cloud faded as rapidly as it came with Paul. Pastor Longstreet had not witnessed his arrival. Now he was leaving. Paul was gone. Grant pondered what had transpired, but rational thought eluded him. His thoughts went to the kid that he had harmed all those years ago. *How sorry I am, and please forgive me,* he thought. He fell upon his knees, which appeared to be revitalized, and began to pray.

The eyes that were bright and full of life fought off a sudden challenge to stay awake. Grant stood and immediately sat down in his well-worn recliner. He thought maybe he was having a heart attack, and looked around for his black telephone, an object that his visitors wanted him to discard.

"Grant, I am sent to you by God. He is tasking you with a great gift."

Grant wanted to talk, but his mind could not formulate any questions. He observed the giant figure clad in white and radiat-ing. It was difficult to discern any details because the being glowed brightly, and staring forced his eyes downward.

"In two days, you must gather in the town's Convention Center and request that there is media coverage. You must also give away all your tangible possessions as you will have no further need of them. Prepare your final message for the people. Tell them of the glory of God."

Grant asked, "Why do I need media coverage?"

The angel continued without answering, "The sermon that you will deliver will eventually be heard by the entire world. From Israel to Rome to Africa and to all people that inhabit the earth. Missionaries in remote regions will deliver the sermon. Christian teachers, who have an ear, shall deliver your sermon. You must announce to them that they should give away their personal possessions and follow you. Remove your doubt and follow a bright glow in the distance that you alone shall see. Your followers shall grow, and they will come from all corners of the earth, they will follow because they have been chosen, but not all. The Great Deceiver shall cause malevolence among your followers for he is always seeking souls to devour. His assault shall pour out a venom that will poison the souls of the doubters, and will be a deep thorn in your side. Fear not and follow the light for God's host will be at your command."

Pastor Longstreet spoke, "Sir, I am old and require assistance to live day to day. My physical body is worn from the years of being alive."

"All infirmities that you had have been cast aside," spoke the angel. "You have been reborn and shall move undeterred."

The angel still sensed the doubt. "Do you believe that the Lord God is omnipresent, and the Bible is the inspired Word of God?"

"I do, my lord."

"Then just rely on your faith, which will be all that you need. You have witnessed the work of God today on multiple occasions and you still doubt. Marvel at the many that will follow your lead just by invoking the Word of God. To whom much is given, much shall be expected," continued the angel.

"Following your message, you shall pass by the people and seek the light that shall be your beacon. Don't tarry, because the minions of hate shall attempt to delay your journey. You will witness the fury of the devil. He has no control over you. Your doubt will open ave-nues for evil to covertly gain ground. Call on the Lord God, and your way shall be cleared. Go now and continue your rest and you shall be awakened when tomorrow calls. Paul came to you as a human brother for he is human, less spiritual than you, but unbelieving, as you are."

The angel departed, and Pastor Longstreet fell into a deep, soothing sleep. His dreams were filled with the pleasantries of his life. He had no present worries.

CHAPTER 17

Sleep was not comforting lately for Paul. He was constantly being tormented by the unholy minions of the devil. They attacked his mind, they outright lied, and they transformed into familiar beings that kept him wondering who he was. When he called on the Christ, they fluttered away. Being constantly tormented by these denizens of darkness was difficult because his mind was constantly under assault, like ripples in oceans that dispersed when brushed aside but imme-diately returned when left alone. These miscreants were not so easily brushed away.

His mission he understood, but where it was leading, he remained perplexed. He knew that there would be a reckoning. He only hoped that he would stand tall. The things that had transpired recently was an adventure manifested on pages in a novel. A melo-drama that was all real, no fiction.

Daniel and Rebecca knocked repeatedly on his door. "Open up, we know you are in there. I have a key," exclaimed Daniel. "Open up or we will."

"Okay, give me a second. Don't you two need some personal time together?"

"We have all the time in the world, just open the door." Paul's friends barged into his apartment, not waiting for an invi-tation or further acknowledgment. They were dressed and apparently were ready to travel.

"Come on, Paul, let's get some breakfast at the corner diner. We haven't seen much of you lately."

"You know that I have been busy."

Interrupting him, Daniel said, "Yeah, yeah, we know." They laughed in unison while barging into his room, which lacked luster but was covered with numerous sports memorabilia.

"What are you doing inside on this lovely day? Let's go to the mall and catch a show," Daniel suggested.

"I am awaiting a call," he responded.

"Listen, if you can receive a call here, you can receive a call at the mall. This is the twentieth century, and that cell phone which you have can receive calls from around the world. The mall is only down the street."

"Okay, I can't argue with that." He laughed.

"My man."

"Stop that madness." They laughed together.

Rebecca played with the television remote, seeking some other channel besides sports. "Clean this joint up." Rebecca laughed, tossing clothes into a pile. "Want me to clean this place later at a greatly increased price?" she continued. "This is getting better all the time."

"Better than what?" inquired Paul.

Daniel walked around the apartment remembering how Lena had given it life, but the life of the apartment appeared to have left with her. Rebecca and Daniel took a seat. Paul watched Rebecca's eyes appearing to pierce Daniel. She was urging him to ask the ques-tion that had brought them to the apartment.

"Hey, bro," inquired Daniel, "tell me why you believe in God. We were never overtly religious or even ever showed any inclination to the church." He spoke freely. "What has changed?"

"You remember when we spoke earlier about what has hap-pened to me and what has appeared to change me? Well, I remember being in Senegal, Africa, while in the war, on this trip sponsored by Morale, Welfare and Recreation. On a boat going to Gorée Island, an island where the imprisoned slaves were gathered to be sent to the Americas, there was a lady, an evangelist, who asked me if I knew the Lord Jesus

Christ as my Lord and Savior." Paul looked directly at his friends and continued. He watched as they paid total attention to his spoken words.

"She innocently, but tenaciously, pursued me and explained the story of salvation. When I returned to Germany, several unknown people, at least I did not know them, invited me to church for various functions and activities. They approached me and began talking about God. I thought it to be a coincidence at first, but the repeated urging caused me to wonder about Jesus Christ. That weekend, I went into the church, and following the service, I took Christ into my life." Hesitating, he continued, "And remember when I was agonizing over losing this ring that Lena had given me? After days of looking, I asked God if he would help me find the crazy ring. You know that Lena would have felt hurt if I had lost that ring. You will not believe this."

"Just finish," said Daniel, as he watched his friend conclude.

"I placed my hand on the floor and touched the ring. You know I had diligently investigated the lost ring situation all week. This seems odd, but I started thinking that if God would do such an inconsequential thing for me, what would he do for the devout? So that kind of gave credibility to my new way of life." Paul just smiled. "That is incredulous that you have tied this conversion to today. Simply crazy, but I respect you, bro. Like always, I am one hundred percent with you."

Then, oddly, Rebecca asked, "How can we gain this salvation?" "You know I am no pastor or qualified person to confer any-thing on anyone, but I think you have to just ask."

CHAPTER 18

As Paul and his friends departed his apartment, he envisioned how beautiful Lena had been swimming in her thoughts, reminiscing how she was overwhelmingly happy when they were together. A swirl of joy floated her on her feet across the street. Her laugh was hypno-tizing and captivating. She had found joy, and her personal demons now lay low. Lena had said, "This is life", while prancing around Paul as they walked. She was incredibly happy. In her mind, she was in a different reality.

During the drive, Paul recollected how he asked Daniel if he thought that marriage enhanced his life. Daniel smiled and had responded with an emphatic, "Yes!"

Daniel said, "What are you asking me, dude? Are you talking marriage?" They laughed at the time, but a truth had been revealed, that soon would have been answered.

CHAPTER 19

Paul turned the key upon return to his apartment and his mind wandered again to Lena. They had looked in every window on the crowded street, and they imagined owning everything they saw and casting away those things that were a bit ostentatious. They fre-quently walked the city streets window shopping.

He had fumbled with the ring box secreted in his pocket. He wanted to hand it to her, but his reticence was heightened. *What if she refused the ring?* he thought. Perspiration was consuming him. *Later, later.* Being embarrassed on the street would be humiliating.

"What are you fumbling with in your pocket, dear one?" Her voice resonating in his brain.

"Nothing," he replied. His nerves had thwarted his courage. "There has to be something rumbling in that complex mind of yours. Not baseball scores." She laughed.

Two pieces of wheat bread, cheese, turkey, and he had dinner. Coupled with a diet soda, he was certain that the evening would be okay. Unless Daniel or Rebecca bugged him, he would enjoy the evening alone.

Paul removed his tennis shoes and lay on the couch, searching his television for some sporting event, other than those which he was not fond of watching. After finding one that pleased him, he became enthralled.

He loved all the Pittsburgh sporting teams and the Oklahoma City basketball team. So finding something he wanted to watch was not difficult. Track and field, golf, karate, and boxing. Something was always on.

CHAPTER 20

The auditorium was a community center that served as a town meet-ing center. Many events occurred within the large room. Everyone in the city had been there numerous times.

Cushioned seats arranged in rows and columns met the attend-ees as they arrived. They were set out carefully to allow for the attendees to enjoy maximum comfortable space. People mingled and exchanged pleasantries. They laughed and gave no indication that whatever Pastor Longstreet was going to say would not be disconcert-ing or alarming. He was a good man, loved by the entire city. Many thought he would ask for money or update them on the progress of the new church, maybe the investigation into the church burning.

Still milling around in the auditorium, Pastor Longstreet qui-eted the crowd as they claimed available seats. A cameraman from one of the TV stations set his operations into use. What was strange was that Grant, normally clad in suits and rarely out of them, appeared before them clad in khaki pants with a noncolorful poncho draped over his shoulders. He did not appear to be the feeble man hindered by age, but seemed transformed into a vibrant figure, newly ener-gized. He moved directly to the podium with many acknowledg-ments, seemingly more interested in getting this meeting started and over with.

Grant struggled with some cards that he placed on the podium. He looked out at the many faces that he had known for over forty years. His eyes stared at the gleaming faces that were receiving him. "In the name of the Living God, let us pray. Father in heaven, let me deliver this message that thou have requested that I deliver. Our time, the time of the Gentiles has ended, and the trials of the Book of Revelation is upon us."

The many people looked toward the pastor, seemingly surprised at the beginning of the message.

Grant continued, "I must admit a discretion that has haunted me over the years. When I was young, I took part in a disgraceful event where a gang of us children assaulted a black youth and severely harmed him. He remains paralyzed by that event. I am profoundly hurt, and no verbal apology can totally recompense for the evil that was perpetrated that hideous day."

"When we are not loving, not caring for our neighbors as God has asked, we fall from the glory of God. The God that I have failed still entrusts me with an even greater task. Give the glory to God."

People began to mill around in their chairs, occasionally glanc-ing about. They were not certain what was going to be said or asked of them. The movement settled.

"Dear brothers and sisters, white, black, brown, and yellow and anyone that I might have forgotten, God loves you." There were few people in attendance that were not white. "He has directed me to admonish everyone of the time of troubles that are at your doorsteps. Because he loves you, he wants you to hear me. Those that hear me will see, those that do not hear me, shall remain blind."

"In God's kingdom there are only the children of men that have been glorified by his Word. There are no Baptist, Lutherans, Catholics, Episcopalians, or any other denominations that divide believers. The educated and unlearned, the poor and the rich gather together in harmony. There is only the family of God. One people, one land, and one love. No one weeps or wails, no hate, only love, brothers and sisters in Christ. The time is upon us. Do not wait behind, or hoard belongings. Give away all that you have and follow me on the journey that awaits. By faith, I am following the Word of God, and by faith, you should also follow."

Maybe the artificial lighting or the sun's rays, a glow encom-passed the old pastor. The gathering had their concerns, and many mumbled because they were uncertain what was being said. A few people gathered their belongs but did not leave. Being on the cusp of leaving, they listened attentively.

"I want to make it clear what God is asking of you. I want there to be no doubts in your mind. Many of you have achieved status amongst your family and friends. You have amassed great fortunes and wealth. You enjoy the fruits of your labor, but the time is com-ing, and it has arrived. They are worthless." He paused. "Cast them aside and follow me on this journey that God requires of you."

The gathering became restless, and the comments by their reli-gious leader, a pastor that had been with them for all their lives, became disconcerting. They wondered if he was serious. Did he mean for them to sell or cast aside their fortune to travel to some remote area? Does God actually speak to man? What of the abomi-nation of desolation spoken of by the prophet Daniel? What were the other prophecies that would forecast the end of times?

CHAPTER 21

The trauma of the church's burning, the overwhelming times, cer-tainly these events had disturbed the pastor's rational thinking. An elderly gentleman attempted to interrupt the broadcast. He would not allow his friend and pastor to suffer undue assailing by the multitude.

"Jim, I love you as much as anyone on this planet. Gather your peace. The intellectual debates and the Bible studies have come to fruition. Believe me that I am speaking today as commanded by our God." His friend regained his seat, although somewhat reluctantly.

Someone shouted, "Be clear! What are you saying and what do you want?"

"I want nothing. It is your God that commands that you be obedient to his Word. Leave your worldly belongings and follow me." Grant watched with a heavy heart as the attendees, many life-long friends, began to leave the auditorium. He knew he had not prepared them totally for this time and wanted God to forgive them because he lacked the knowledge that would have joined them with God.

Take care, my brother. You have delivered the message that was requested of you, a soothing voice attempted to encourage him. Now go to the location of the burned church and wait. Remain in prayer, take no food or aid. A long and tedious journey beckons you. God will prepare your body for this arduous journey. Go in peace. Our friend will meet with you soon, explained the peaceful whispering.

As the crowd departed, the demonic emissaries found fertile soil. "He has gone crazy. He listens to the darkness. Get away from him now.

How far has he fallen?" They laughed while tormenting the crowd that thirty minutes earlier had revered this man of God. People mumbled obscenities, which had been enhanced by the demonic attacks. "He is out of his old crazy mind."

Grant, whose eyes fought the tears that wanted expression, slowly moved from behind the podium. "I have failed God again, and hope that Satan will not prey upon them because of me."

"Too late, Pastor, they are within reach now and shall join our leader soon. You cannot expect these hardworking people to give up their savings blindly. Our army grows every second, and soon we will harvest even you."

"In the name of Jesus Christ, get behind me, Satan." The tor-ment stopped immediately, allowing Grant to ponder his last com-mand from the unknown holy voice. Go to the burned church.

Grant did not linger on the stares and the unfriendly gazes that followed him. The sheriff turned away as he walked past him.

A cool spring wind swept across the valley as steam appeared to ooze from Grant's person. He was alone, and his many friends that had praised him earlier were gone. They would have given him anything within their means. That was hours ago. Now alone on the hill, he wondered what had happened and what was in store. He began to pray.

CHAPTER 22

An unexplained earthquake rattled St. Louis, Missouri, resulting in thousands of deaths. A tornado leveled a portion of Houston, Texas, and the Colosseum in Rome began to burn. Nature had unexpec-tantly assaulted the wonders of men. The television stations and their weather channels were inundated with news of sudden deadly catastrophes, and their weather experts explained each event with coherency.

Crime gained a new impetus, and criminals appeared to claim the streets while battered first responders withered under the societ-ies' apparent collapse. A plea for patience and reason appeared to be met with deaf ears. Society had bordered on chaos, and the unknown, unholy minions were drunk with the taste of the calamity.

Political leaders who had once attempted to blame the indi-gent for unlawfulness were taken aback because all status of society engaged in the calamity. There were no religions, races, ethnic affil-iations that were immune. Society was in turmoil, trying to regain a semblance of normalcy. This was a worldwide phenomenon. No place on the planet had sanctuary; all suffered in kind.

Sheriff John Pickney attentively listened to news feeds and watched the sudden events of the day transpire. He had been vigilant and posted a deputy to perform surveillance where the fallen pastor sat.

This town would not fall victim to the sudden phenomena of abnormal events. He would be proactive in his efforts to abruptly halt any discontent within the town. All available deputies were on standby or working extended shifts to keep the town in order.

Pickney remembered Grant's admission of criminal activity as a youth and decided to send an official inquiry to the nation's intelligence community to obtain further adverse information, if available.

One had to be proactive to offset those that worshipped disor-der. He would not fail on his watch. Grant was a friend, but now he did not know him. A true friend surreptitiously under his radar for many years. "You just never know anyone," he mumbled out loud.

"Look how that old man played you like a fool. You're a very polite, caring man," the voice was vindictive. "You have always held him in high esteem. You have dined with him. He knows your fam-ily, and you have taken special care to cater to him. Look how he repays your friendship. Just a chump," the voice continued. "You can't trust people in your position, because look how you are repaid. Why did he not alert you to what he had planned? You could have spoken with him. But no. Sucker."

Pickney fumed, "Never again."

The voice was encouraging. "Keep a close eye on him. You will get your revenge." The soothing suggestions appeared to have form. A shadow appeared and dissipated.

CHAPTER 23

Grant was truly alone now. Forty odd years had been for nothing. He was not just an old fool. *You are correct, dear man. You are just a fool.* Temptation assaulted him and manifested itself, peering sorrowfully and standing like a stone wall before him.

He continued, *Live, Grant, enjoy the riches awaiting you. My mas-ter doesn't wish you pain and infamy. He only desires that you stand with him. All your friends will return, and you can immediately regain your status. It is all in your hands, and a simple affirmation of his authority will return you to your way of life.*

"Get behind me, Satan, in the name of Jesus!" Grant closed his eyes, and his thoughts slipped into a place where better times returned anew. The demon's emissary had vanished.

The darkness of the day was rapidly giving way to the night, and the pastor could only wonder why he had been chosen. Chosen for what he could not contemplate, but now more ready to begin. If evil has taken time to sway him from his assignment, it must be worth his tenacity to stand firm.

A man appeared before him; he was taller than anyone he knew. His features were unblemished and his physique powerful. He nei-ther smiled nor appeared sullen.

"Pastor, please stand, for I come from God." He reached out a hand to help Grant to his feet. With only a slight tug, Grant faced him.

Grant's height of six feet three inches was still at least two feet shorter than this strange man. Grant stood and backed up slightly.

"Do not fear me, Preacher, your day in paradise awaits you. But God has chosen you to complete an important assignment." He stared intently at Grant. "There will be a holy light always in your distance. Follow the beacon as it will be a light, a sun to you, and the others cannot see. The travel will be perilous with many obsta-cles, but heed… have no fear. Your flock that follows you will run away. Some will fall along the road, others will believe the minions of darkness, who will be as constant plagues. They have no control over you, so do not despair. Don't tarry longer than necessary at any place. Offer no one promises as they will not be fulfilled. Give no payments, because they will be paid. Give no one special favors for the poor and the rich are the same. Seek not nourishment, for they will be nourished. God is the God of Abraham, Isaac, and Jacob, and the God of Israel. Take heed, the light shines in the west."

"Where are the others?" he nervously asked.

"Do not worry about those that once loved and adored you. Remember, it is difficult for those who claim to know you to believe you, for you will not be honored in your own home, but they who have heard your voice today, even now prepare to join you."

"Where am I leading them?" he inquired.

The angel faded away and left with one last admonishment. "Follow the light."

Paul replaced the angel and smiled. "The light angel wanted me to assure you this is no dream or hoax. I was much like you a few months ago. Now I have no concerns, just uncertain of what will transpire."

"This is all so odd. Why was I chosen?" Grant asked.

"I had the same questions and concerns. I just move with each assignment now," said Paul.

"These are strange days indeed," responded Pastor Longstreet.

"Yes, sir, I will see you soon," replied Paul. As before, he faded as he arrived, into the cloud.

With nothing to gather, and by faith alone, Pastor Longstreet sought out the light. He did not look back, and gave Stewart, Virginia, no further concerns.

CHAPTER 24

Lena removed from the hanger her lovely gown that she wanted to wear at her wedding. She had purchased it months ago, certain that she would, in her near future, adorn this elegant dress. She had taken Rebecca with her, who was overwhelmed that Lena would finally find the happiness that she sought.

As much as Rebecca had reaped praise on her lifelong friend, it had been in vain. Rebecca's ruminations remained reticent until she met Paul. She had finally found someone destined for her friend.

It was love at first sight; however, the equally introverted Paul hindered this union. Years passed but nothing, not even casual talk, frequent dinners, and movies, had been a catalyst. But at the least possible place for a union, a nightclub, things had changed. A date alone.

How fate had weaved its wand. Best friends and best friends. They lived in the same building, worked at the same place in differ-ent sections, and were frequently together.

Lena had given Paul a quick kiss, told him she would see him later and that she was extremely tired.

No effort to light the apartment, Lena slowly walked into her bedroom. Her mind captive to her fears, constantly exposing her to the negatives that ran her life. *Paul does not really care for me and I know I am ugly. I just continue to be a burden to all my friends.* She sat on her bed and lit several candles. She rose and undressed.

Lena gathered over a hundred OxyContin, cupped them into her hand, and swallowed the entire lot, chased with a diet Coke. She would soon join her parents, who died while she was in college.

Lena gazed upon her wedding gown and began to dress. She slipped on her shoes and placed the tiara on her head. She penned a letter to Rebecca.

> My dearest friend, no…sister,
>
> Why God decided to send me a more loving friend than I ever deserve, I don't know. You have been the light in my dark life. When others have shunned me, you have always comforted me with love. I am profoundly grateful. I love you.
>
> This life is far too difficult to live in for me. You found me the love of my life, who I love as much as I love you, but why should I torment him? He would live an unenjoyable life always caring for me while forgoing his life. That I can-not allow.
>
> I guess this has always been on my mind. However, your friendship has prolonged my life and this fate. Somehow, if I had never known you, I would have left this place long ago.
>
> Give my love to Daniel, and mostly to Paul.
>
> You know I love you. Forever, my love.

Lena blew out the candles and waited for the chilling call of death. She yawned several times and drifted into a peaceful slumber.

A powerful angel with a flaming sword barred her way. Without speaking, he pointed a finger to a large bridge, directing her onward. She paused, he then stated, "Go!"

She crossed the stone bridge, slowly glancing to her sides, and directly to her front. There were many figures on the other side. They were awaiting judgment and now they welcomed another soul. Their thought had long ago nulled in their minds. They had no opinions about anything. Silently waiting their fate.

"I have been calling Lena any number of times, without any response." Rebecca was swiping away Daniel's searching hands. "Where is that girl?"

"You know she is probably with Paul, window shopping," responded Daniel.

"She still would answer her cell phone for me," she replied.

"Call Paul," interjected Daniel.

"No, I am going to her apartment." Rebecca gathered the keys for Lena's apartment and departed. The short trip to Lena's apartment she traversed quickly. She rang the bell and listened for noise.

Daniel called Paul, who did not answer his cell phone.

Yeah, yeah, you devil, Daniel immediately thought.

Rebecca entered a dark apartment, which was very strange, because Lena did not like the complete darkness. She fumbled around searching for the light switch, attempting to recall the loca-tion of the few pictures that Lena had hung. Finally, finding one, she switched it on.

CHAPTER 25

Angel Concepcion tended goats together with his trusted dog herder named Coyote. Enjoying the simple life which freed him of any responsibilities, even if it was for a small time. His life was simple, but his responsibilities were many. The alone time away from his family and friends gave him time to think and reflect on life in general.

The brown sun-hardened dirt appeared to lack life; however, it sustained him and his family. Care had to be taken with growing food; constant watering was required and proper nurturing. Hard life gave proper training for living, he had been told numerous times by his father, who had passed long ago.

Angel wiped the sweat off his brow and inhaled deeply. The perspiration soaking into his shirt gave a cooling effect when the wind blew. He loved this life.

What would he preach on this Sunday? he thought. Coyote, his dog, walked alongside him, keeping a vigilant eye on the herd. *Maybe the glory of living in whatever circumstances one found themselves.* In all circumstances one would find comfort if it were sought in earnest. Those who constantly suffered, self-created or forced upon them, would find themselves in a better situation in the next life. Smiling, his concerns were relaxed.

A small Gila monster scrambled after a scorpion that tried to evade his pursuer. His destiny determined, he turned toward his prey and defiantly offered resistance.

Several tumble weeds rambled freely in many directions, offer-ing no resistance. Wherever they bounced across the plain was where they should be at this specific time and place. *What freedom,* he thought.

Lost in his thoughts, he had not immediately seen the six strang-ers that crossed the undulating dust hills to his front. They walked without speech and moved away from him as they passed. Their rag-ged khaki-colored clothes danced in the resurfacing wind. An odious sulfuric smell announced their presence.

The group stopped and turned. They faced Angel, who had stopped, his facial appearance heightened by a blank stare, his eyes enlarged. "Hello," spoke Angel.

They did not reply.

"Is there something you need?" asked Angel. "There is a small town toward the east and only desert to the west."

Still, they did not speak.

Angel watched as they transformed. White translucent deformed beings sneered toward him. Their expressions, void of emotions, glared.

An invading, encompassing fear overcame him. He wanted to run to escape this unholy torment. It challenged his reality. Without thought, he grasped his gold religious cross that hung around his neck. Coyote whined, seeking refuge at his feet. The goat herd still plodded on oblivious to all.

He was a preacher, an acolyte of the Living God. These abomi-nations had no control over him. He remembered when he was much younger how he was able to recognize the unholy occupying human forms. These grotesque beings, unknowing to the person, had their souls possessed. And the possessed gave no resistance.

Angel prayed often, asking God to free him of this torment. He wanted his soul free. When he was younger, these demonic forms were ever present and superimposed over human bodies. They rec-ognized him, but never engaged him. They appeared to sneer, but averted confrontation. As he aged, they disappeared altogether, and he was pleased.

Now, they had returned, and he wondered why. Had he dis-pleased God in some way? His immediate concern was these six aber-rations. He was taken aback that there were no human hosts. What had changed?

As rapidly as they appeared, they departed. They sneered, and within their faces he observed the inherent hatred. Their forms dis-sipated. Why had they come? What had changed? he asked himself again.

CHAPTER 26

Jeb Lee sat quietly, reading his morning newspaper, fumbling with a cup filled with steaming black coffee. As he sipped from the ceramic cup, he quickly removed his lips, avoiding a scalding. "Ah," he said, relishing the taste. He loved the aroma that tantalized his mind. Happy to be awake and dealing with the new challenges of the day. He lived a good life.

He sat quietly, glancing toward the television and occasionally peering out of his kitchen window adorned with extended white drapes that teased the shining hardwood floors that were throughout his home. His furniture was totally mixtures of creams and whites and had been carefully coordinated by his wife. Pictures hung in all the rooms, and most reflected very scenic landscapes.

It reflected Southern beauty with European charm. Several valuable antiques highlighted the rooms, which harmoniously stood amid a serene palette of creams and beiges.

His wife had joined him and began preparing breakfast. They exchanged their greetings and sealed their oneness with a kiss.

The TV reported that several black youths were arrested late last night while attempting to rob a convenience store around mid-night. However, a sheriff's deputy car arrived on the scene, and the officer's quick response ended the robbery before it began. All three youths were sixteen and had been taken into custody, awaiting future arraignments. The television announcer professionally presented the results of the events that past evening. Continuing, the reporter said he was unaware of what led police to arrest the youths. Pastor Lee simply shook his head.

The kitchen was filled with several different aromas, which exacerbated his hunger, which he was now cognizant of while reach-ing for a breakfast roll. It was an immutable fact that his wife's cook-ing was simply delectable.

"Can't ever explain why these people seemed to have an affinity for calamity. I guess only God knows," Jean Lee, the pastor's wife, offered without solicitation. She was just removing several slices of bacon and placing them neatly on Jeb's plate. There were two eggs fried hard, two rolls, and a side of grits. This was a hardy meal that would get her husband fueled for the day.

The TV announcer continued with his newscast. A local family of five was found dead in their rural home. There had not been con-firmation of what transpired, but it appeared to be a family-related incident. A suicide note and the evidence support that this was an internal incident. The Lee family made no acknowledgment of this incident.

Nationally, a twenty-year-term pastor in California had been removed from his church for introducing a radical alternative mes-sage not supported by the church. Apparently, the radical preaching had splintered this mega church. After deliberation and consider-ation for the tenured pastor, the church leadership had stripped him of all his responsibilities and a new pastor was being sought.

Additionally, on the national front, six members of a hate group had been killed following an early morning raid at their location. Further, the vehicle and four of the members responsible for the recent terror activity on the inhabitants of the church in Baltimore, Maryland, were identified. The police did not disclose how they were identified, but stated that the investigation was ongoing. The vehicle in which they escaped was recovered.

Jeb, using the remote, turned off the television as he prepared to bless the food. "Lord, bless the preparers and providers of this food. In Jesus's name we pray, amen." With his spouse, they ate their breakfast with small, short exchanges that spanned a range of topics.

A yellow tabby crossed the floor occasionally, announcing his presence with a soft "meow".

"Jean," said Jeb, "I had this strange dream last night. This is a bit embarrassing."

Jean noted the reluctance, but looking directly at him, she urged him on without saying anything. His nervousness was obvious, but he continued. "There in front of me and seemingly oblivious were two great beastly beings engaged in a guttural conversation. Many more appeared, but they were scattered some distance from the two that were nearby. The two that were close appeared to look in my direction and smile. They continued their exchange and continued to occasionally glance to where I stood. Beckoning me forward, the larger of the two cast images of profound desires in my mind. He laughed as these forbidden thoughts appeared lifelike in front of me, but their vivid presentations were filling my mind. The two beings never moved, nor did the surroundings change. I had a strong urge to run, but I seemed to be bound to the place by a chained mind."

He reached for Jean's hand, seeking comfort during his remembrance of this ghastly ordeal. "Those beings turned toward me and appeared to beckon me forward. I pushed back to distance myself from them, but I remained embedded in place. I thought I was about to die from sheer terror when I was engulfed in a very bright light."

"From the light emanated a voice, calm and peaceful, 'Fear not, Jeb, the Lord has work for you to do. I am his messenger that is pav-ing the way for the light.' The glow seemed to ebb from bright to a dimmer light, kind of oscillating in and out. 'There will be a man who will come to you tomorrow and he will explain the dream.'"

"I immediately woke reaching for you to ensure myself that I was amongst the living. I was totally startled, to say the least. I rolled out of bed and came to the kitchen, where you found me earlier watching television."

"What a strange dream. I wonder if you had possibly eaten something which had not agreed with you."

"Do not know," he replied while finishing off a slice of crisp bacon. "It was so vivid and real. It was like I was actually there, horrified, until the light revealed itself. It was like I was in hell with many demons." He sipped his coffee.

A knock at the door returned him to his immediate reality. Jeb glanced at the clock and noticed that it was early morning. The colorful clockface displayed 8:30 a.m. "Who could that be?" he said as he stood. He, out of habit, tugged at the belt that secured his house robe. He was not sure who it could be and channeled his mind to task. Had he scheduled a meeting? I don't think so, he subconsciously answered his question.

Pastor Jeb viewed this recently installed device that monitored the outside of his house and readily concluded that the person at the door was a stranger. He had intended not to answer the door, but the tone rang again. He was a bit surprised to determine that the visitor was black. He struggled to recall when a black person had come to his door. Other than a mailman, there had been none. He treated the mailman respectfully and had occasionally enjoyed a brief cordial conversation.

The humid warm morning air assaulted Jeb as it sought entrance into the cooled home. It was trying to seek a temporary respite from the imminent heat that tended to dominate the area for extended periods of time. Several neighbors employed regular help to maintain their manicured lawns and homes. Jeb noticed them, and certainly they would notice this uninvited visitor. He would answer questions later he knew would arise when he met his neighbors later in the day. The domestics, who often acted as security, would provide a detailed briefing of what they had observed to their employers, all the time hoping to gain favor from them. They were the eyes and ears of the neighborhood. Their grapevine network readily alerted the natural residents of events that deviated from the regular events within the area.

"How may I help you?" asked Jeb.

CHAPTER 27

Paul slept peacefully for hours and dreamed of his field of life, a tranquil world where life and harmony were synonymous. He reveled in this world of bliss and enjoyed the countless times that he had visited. There were no challenges here, just repetitious feelings of joy that never faded. He had been bestowed a great honor by the Living God and was always overwhelmed in this world. It was like the most pleasurable place one could define.

The angel of light interrupted his tranquility, and the dream brought on new wonders. "Wake," the commanding voice of the angel called to Paul. Even the voice, although stern, did not change his mood. "Awake."

Paul's consciousness submitted to the command. "I am here, my lord," he replied.

With the light came the darkness. The hellish demons were held in abeyance by the radiance of the angel. They wanted to torment Paul, but burned in the light, and as they scurried back, they offered insults, but they were immediately set aflame by the light.

Bigger demons stayed far back to avoid the resulting confla-gration. They shouted blasphemies and indignities, they hissed and cursed, but they had not grown by engaging the light. The light then became so brilliant that the interlopers were no more.

Paul stood and held his head slightly bowed; however, the light spoke to him. "We are servants of our God. We are the same in his eyes. Raise your head high, for God has truly blessed you to carry out his works. I am of the heavenly realm and you are of the earth. We live to honor God."

The light encircled him, and the light became increasingly brighter. "The darkness is insidious and seek to delay their reckon-ing. You shall go to Savannah, Georgia, and speak with another ser-vant of God. He is a pastor by trade, a speaker of the Word. God is not happy with him and wants you to speak with him and admonish him of his shortcomings. Tell him that the Lord has found him want-ing and his soul shall soon be required," replied the light.

The light observed the sadness in Paul, and sought to give him encouragement. "God wants you to offer the pastor a choice between life and death. His appointed time was determined from his birth. The choice where he remains is his. You are God's earthly emissary, and much is required of you. Even now the darkness tugs at your heart. Seek the treasures that await you in the light."

The landscape was breathtaking, decorated with tall moss-cov-ered oak trees whose canopy cast a natural sheltering cover from the bright sunlight. The Victorian-styled homes with their huge bay windows decorated the streets and appeared to remain unchanged for centuries. The unmistaken beauty of the city was comparable to any other more prominently mentioned.

Stepping tentatively through the cloud, Paul had again jour-neyed hundreds of miles in seconds. He was unsteady but by now assured that he would pass quickly through the mist without any unexpected occurrences. *Follow the light,* the words rang softly in his mind.

Paul stood quietly at the corner of two intersecting streets. The lawns along the streets had been catered to by the employed neighborhood workers who were diligently carrying out their daily tasks. They observed as he casually looked toward where they worked. He wondered, had they seen him emerge from the cloud? The workers did not appear startled, but kept a lower gaze in his direction.

Crows appeared to gather more abundantly above. The robins and sparrows sought their way free from the area as they sensed the arrival of something amiss. Although there did not appear any darkening clouds, moments earlier a light darkness suddenly appeared. Unearthly beings and abominations flooded the area, hissing and blaspheming. They flew to and fro, subliminally assaulting everyone they saw. The workers became angry and argued with one other. The demons laughed loudly. They relished tormenting people who always found fault in each other.

The demons' attention returned to the tasks they had been assigned. They had greater prey, and now focused their attention toward Paul and Pastor Jeb. They would have overwhelmed the two had it not been for legions of God's warriors that surrounded Paul and Jeb. The warriors' glow forced the adversary slowly backward. Even the calling birds fluttered away. Sunlight piercing the over-head canopy regained its dominance. The arguments that had arisen slowly subsided.

The warriors' leader, a bright emerging light, hovered above Paul and Jeb. He raised his hand, and the demons scurried at remark-able speed, wanting to avoid the glance of the greater light. But they only scurried far enough away to remain out of sight. They knew they would gain audience again with Pastor Jeb and his wife after God's warriors departed. They were not totally aware of why Paul was there, but their patience would be rewarded, then their actions could be properly directed. But while the great light barrier was there, they were forced to acquiesce, or face immediate judgment and be sent directly to hell. Their ultimate destiny was in the pits of hell.

"Sir, my name is Paul, and I am on a mission given to me by God. He has sent me to explain to you a mission that the Lord has designated for you."

"Who is it, honey?" a soft Southern-accented voice asked.

"I am not certain myself," he replied.

Having now entered the front of the home and noticing that a black man stood at the door, Jean spoke, "Should I contact the authorities, dear?"

"No, I don't believe that will be necessary at this moment."

Jean, now conscious that she was wearing her house robe, tugged it tightly around her body. A Southern lady should not be seen wearing less than what was historically proper. And yes, this was a black man, a member of people known for giving in to their very desires and with insatiable lust.

Standing silently, observing these godly people encapsulated by stereotypes and innuendos, Paul wondered to himself, *If followers of God are so fearful of people they do not know, how does anyone expect the nonbeliever to act otherwise?*

"Again, God has sent me to you to deliver a message." Paul noticed that Jeb appeared to be thinking and searching for a response. "Pastor Lee, do not fear me. I am not your enemy, but I am sure the enemy is not far."

"What enemy?" Jeb replied nervously.

"Your enemy and mine, the Prince of Darkness."

Raising his voice slightly, Jeb asked, "The devil?"

"One and the same."

Jean had come alongside of Jeb by now and was holding tightly to her cell phone. "Should I call the police?" she asked.

Jeb held her hand now.

She became cognizant of how she was attired standing at the door. The workers were obviously looking toward them now with more interest. They feigned work and cast a wayward eye. They were far less interested in their jobs and more on the stranger and the pastor.

Paul began to realize that this was becoming awkward and wanted to deescalate the inquiring eyes. "Is there a better time and location that we can meet?"

"I don't have much free time today to meet," Jeb quickly added. "My time today is clearly all taken."

"I must talk with you today and soon. Your time and life on earth is short."

"Is that some sort of threat?" Jeb asked, becoming frustrated.

"By no means, sir," replied Paul. "However, your time is short."

"Short?" His face became flustered. "Short! I have spoken all that I will right now. Jean, contact the authorities, please."

Paul continued, "Your daughter will call you in ten minutes, and she shall tell you how afraid she was a few weeks ago when she unexpectedly encountered two black youths. She will say how disap-pointed she was with her actions. I will leave now. Please meet with me at noon at the church where you are the pastor."

"Hello, this is Jean Lee, 1860 Jackson Way. There is a black man here at my door harassing us, my husband, Pastor Jeb Lee, and myself. Will you send an officer over, please?"

"Ma'am, remain calm. Does he have any weapons? Is anyone hurt? A unit is en route. Goodbye."

An unexpected comforting breeze eased into the room where Jean stood, holding firmly to the telephone. A voice that was so pleas-ant whispered to her agitated inner being, *Do not consciously interfere with God's plan. Your Christian brother has been directed by God to deliver a message to your husband. He has been asked to bring a message for him to deliver to his brothers. Your husband will not believe him and will have the authorities attempt to upend him. The man, called Paul, will deliver the message but suffer abuse from the authorities. God's plan shall not be delayed or altered.* The unsolicited voice seemed to be fad-ing from her consciousness. The fading voice gave a final statement, *You shall not recall contacting the police. A spiritual event has been set into motion. Time in the spiritual realm cannot be comprehended by God's earthly children. Seconds are minutes, days are months, and years are hundreds of years. What appears to be an extended time on earth, time in the spiritual world is undefined. Countless events transpire every earthly second. We shall speak again soon.*

While the pastor and his wife stood in their doorway, the tele-phone rang. Jean, holding the cell phone, was a bit startled by the sudden telephone call.

The visitor had just disappeared from their sight. They were shocked back into the present by the sounds of the arriving police cruisers. The police arrived quickly, faster than usual.

"Hello? Hello, Mother, this is Mary." "Oh, my dear," Jean said, fumbling with the cell phone and looking at her husband. "Dear, can I call you back in a few minutes?" she asked, a bit flushed by the events.

"Certainly. Mother, is there something wrong? Is Daddy okay?" Mary became excited. Anxiety had suddenly made its presence.

"No, my dear, everyone is fine." The nervousness in her hand and voice overcame her desire to remain calm. She was a bit rat-tled, appearing to be overcome by the unfamiliar man that had been speaking with her husband. *Why was a policeman here?* Jean's mind asked her.

A physically fit police officer approached the pastor and his wife while they stood at their front door. Several other cars arrived, providing him with ample backup should it be needed. "Are you all okay?" he asked.

"Fine, Officer," the reverend replied. He extended his hand.

"What's going on?" asked the police officer.

"There was an unknown black man that was standing here and was discussing something that was very strange. He spoke about how he had been directed by God to speak to me. I just thought that was a bit strange. He did not harm or threaten me."

"Give me a description, please?" asked the officer.

The reverend described him as light brown in skin color, medium build with a mustache and goatee joined. He wore black jeans with a navy-colored shirt and tennis shoes. "He wanted to meet with me at noon at the location where I am the pastor, 1064 Pleasant Avenue."

The officer asked, "Any tattoos or other distinguishing marks?"

"None that I recall, Officer," replied Jeb.

"Give me a moment so that I can send this description out," responded the officer.

"Why are the police here?" asked Jean.

"Don't you remember? You just called them to speak with the stranger at the door."

"I did not call the police," replied Jean.

Pastor Jeb began walking toward the police vehicles. He noticed the faces of his neighbors hidden behind sheer curtains. He knew he would be questioned about these events later. "Jean, I'll speak with the officers at their vehicles. Please finish breakfast," he spoke as he wondered why she had not recalled that she had requested their assistance.

CHAPTER 28

Pastor Lee entered his church, whose doors were always open between 8:00 a.m. and 6:00 p.m. They had no history of anything stolen or any vandalism. Several church officials were always pres-ent, carrying out any number of assignments. A junior official was always assigned to handle daily inquiries and attend to people seek-ing needed counseling.

The people residing in the vicinity of the church were afflu-ent, and unlike many communities, knew nearly 100 percent of the neighborhood inhabitants. There were less than 1 percent of any minority groups residing in that community. Other than the few known minorities, others' presence would always be scrutinized. The police were frequently contacted to interview minorities suspected to be strangers.

For those joyriding, they were immediately admonished to vacate the area. Those that refused most often would be escorted out of the community.

Pastor Lee, at the police officer's suggestion, entered the church assured that plainclothes police officers and detectives would be within and outside of the church. Those that were there for religious reasons had been escorted to a large section of the church that was divided with several individual rooms to commune in silence.

Pastor Lee walked to the first row of wooden pews and sat down. He fumbled with papers retrieved from his briefcase, a solid genuine leather case with his name stenciled on one side along with a large golden cross on the back. Glancing at his watch, he felt relieved that the stranger who confronted him had not arrived.

"Pastor Lee, how are you?" a pleasing voice addressed him.

A bit astonished, Pastor Lee fumbled with any words once he recognized his visitor. Startled a bit, he gathered himself to say "Hi." Recognizing that the people present were as unfamiliar with the church as he was, Paul smiled at Pastor Lee and began, "Sir, the Lord, our God, has a message that he wants you to hear. I have been instructed to inform you that you have been given thirty days to preach the love of God to your parishioners."

Pastor Lee wanted to interject but remained silent. He won-dered why the plainclothes police were not approaching.

"They don't recognize that I am here, so please listen so that you might be judged accordingly. The people that profess their love for God assume that they are being led by an honorable man, a man close to God. You have deceived them and have allowed them to come short of the throne. You allow them to hate their brothers, to judge unfairly, and to honor possessions while the devil counts souls. We fall short, and you have been the instrument of the devil and allowed his minions to run amok in this church."

Pastor Lee responded angrily, "I love God!"

"You do not!" Paul responded in kind. "You love this world and glory in what it gives you, which has been plenty. But God wants me to tell you that he has not forgotten you and shall offer you a chance to guide your church to his many mansions. I have seen them from afar and I bear witness that they exist."

"Which biblical institutions have you attended? Are you Augustinian or Calvin, Baptist or Roman Catholic? Which order do you follow?" inquired Pastor Lee.

"Sir, that information will not help you. Just believe that I am a Christian and sent by God. Please listen. The questions you are ask-ing me will not secure your soul. The devil even now has numbered you among his future minions."

Jeb was frustrated but remained calm. "What do you know about my life and beliefs? I have served and loved God nearly my entire life. I am justified by God. My beliefs justify me."

Paul emphatically shouted, "listen! I am telling you that God is not pleased with your efforts and wants you to change your presen-tation so that all of his children benefit from your teachings, not just a limited few. They are not new creatures, but are of the lost."

"Sir, tell me how I am wanting. Tell me what you believe that I lack."

Paul stared at him directly. "I do not know you and have just met you today. God knows you and he has known you before your birth. He desires that you reside with him eternally."

Pastor Lee said, "I do not believe you," remaining calm. Paul responded, "I have delivered the message from God, just bear with me a bit further. Believe me or not, you must teach the church that they must love their neighbors, whites, blacks, browns, and any others that have accepted the word and teachings of the Christ. Invite those who are different to the church, for this is the church of the Christ."

Small demons surrounded the pastor and tormented his mind with doubt. Pastor Lee sought out God in his thoughts, but was assailed by the demons.

Have we ever led you astray? they muttered. *Who is this? He is not God, just a bum from the streets attempting to interrupt your good deeds. A black man too! Don't listen to him, Pastor.* They honored his title that it would please him.

"You must know that I cannot do that by altering church doc-trine without approval from the deacon board and others affiliated with this church."

Paul said, "Pastor, I struggled internally on what I needed to say to you to make you believe. Your reticence has caused Jesus to bring a profound admonishment upon you. You have seen the things that God has done and yet you still do not believe in the truth that I bring you."

"Well, whoever you really are, I think you might need some mental health counseling. This is nonsense, and I doubt that what you say is true. I have read the Bible, cover to cover, and there is no mention of you."

"Please listen to my last statement to you. God wants you to believe this. Exactly at midnight, your wife shall leave this world. You should give her your undivided attention until she returns to God. There is nothing that I can do to change what has been written by God. I wish I had been more convincing so that this event could have been prevented."

Jeb responded angrily, "Take yourself away from this holy place! There is nothing more that I need to hear!" He stood up and still wondered why the police presence had not interrupted.

The demons tormented the pastor's mind. *Who is he…God? We know God, and that is not him. Slap him for threatening your wife. Such insolence from this black man. You know how they are!*

"Pray to God that he reconsiders, ask him to forgive you and allow you to fulfill the mission that he has given you through me." Paul rose and turned to leave, genuinely believing that he had done his best.

Several large police officers approached Paul. One spoke, "You are under arrest. Place your hands above your head and kneel."

Paul continued on his way as if he had not heard them. He walked without fear, awaiting his cloud that he knew would protect him.

One of the officers shot him repeatedly with his stun gun. The pain of the multiple missiles overcame Paul. The pain was excruciat-ing. He felt he was being pulled across the floor and down the side-walk. He was being thrown into a police cruiser. Several police offi-cers walked back toward the church while others guarded the vehicle.

Paul withered from the pain and wondered why the angel had not come to his aid. He began to doubt the reality that had just trans-pired. The cloud overcame him, and he returned to his room.

CHAPTER 29

"Mary, this is your mother."

"Momma," she replied, "what is going on? How is Dad? Is everything okay?" Mary was startled and needed answers, and she needed them now. "Is everything okay?"

"Everything is just fine, please calm down."

"Let me speak with Dad." Her anxiety was still at the maximum. "He is speaking with the police officer, but everything is fine now." She was more composed now, at least better than her daughter.

"What is going on?" inquired her daughter.

"There was an unknown black man at the door this morning speaking with your father, and it appeared he caused your father some great anxiety. I don't know what the issue was, but your dad was not harmed." Jean passed the telephone from one hand to the other. "He is fine and I believe everything is okay. Oh, here he is."

Jean passed the telephone to Jeb, who was all smiles. "It is your daughter."

"Honey, how are you? Washington is not getting you down, is it? Why is a young girl calling her dad? Shouldn't you be out with your friends?"

"Daddy, I was just calling home when mother mentioned some disturbances outside."

"No, child, just a misunderstanding with some unknown man that had stopped by. He was not causing any special concern, but you never know these days," replied the pastor.

"Are you sure, Daddy? I'll come home right now." Mary fumbled with the telephone, but listening to her dad's voice assured her that he appeared to be out of harm's way. "Well, what are you doing?"

"Gathering the faithful, as always."

Mary broke in, "Did you hear that a pastor on television was asking the faithful to cast away their belongings and follow him? He believes that God has given him direction."

"Yes, it is the current greatest topic spreading through the church. There are several pastors discussing that very same thing. We were a bit taken by surprise." Jeb enjoyed Bible talk. "None of the prophecies have transpired. What would make a veteran pastor speak so haphazardly? Has he examined the scriptures?"

"Yeah, some of the young people are discussing that very same thing. It is popular here around Washington, DC." Mary kicks off her shoes and rubbed her feet. She felt much better now that she was speaking with her dad.

"Okay, I have some work to get done. Don't make yourself a stranger in your own home, young lady."

His light chastisement was all the assurance that Mary needed. "Bye, Dad."

The night was passing slowly by and nothing out of the ordinary occurred. After praying, Jean and Jeb had settled in for the evening. They had shared a good night kiss and gathered the covers. The coolness of the sheets soon gave way to the warmth of their bodies, and the conquering sleep slipped them into a deep comforting bliss. Jean appeared to be wakened as she stood in her bed. Her sleep-

ing husband lay by her, snoring loudly. A very bright light, a light brighter than daylight erupted around her. Surely a dream, thought Jean, until a bright being stood before her with arms opened wide.

The urge to speak was great, but impossible. She supposed a great event was occurring, and the tears that had been harnessed now flowed freely.

The being of bright light spoke, "Child of God, weep not. God is calling you home."

Jean wanted to wake Jeb, but could not.

"Your spouse has been left, and you have entered a new realm in which you cannot leave. You will soon be in the presence of the Majestic God, our God, Jesus Christ. Follow me."

Jean stepped into the brightest light and looked into a chain of continuous happiness. She cried no more.

Jeb slept soundly, wrapped in a warm down comforter. He woke momentarily and watched the clock's arm strike midnight. He slumbered back into a deep sleep, easing himself closer to his wife. Assured that she was still there, he accepted the healing grip of a deep unhindered sleep.

CHAPTER 30

The densely packed woods hid the rising sun far longer than Pastor Longstreet wanted. The canopy was thick, and the sun's light struggled mightily against the natural darkness enhanced by the number of trees and other foliage. Grant observed the light, but his visibility was limited. He gathered small berries, which was a chore since the light had not provided him any assistance. He watched the directing light hover in the distance and waited patiently for the day's journey.

A bird chirped in the distance, which brought on an avalanche of equally similar sounds. The forest began to come alive, announcing the dawning of a new day, which was more immediate than the rising of the sun.

Grant decided to pray and asked that he be worthy of the confidence and trust that was being bestowed upon him, whatever it was. Although the dampness was all around, it had not affected the former pastor. He felt confident that there would not be further events to impede his movement. The lack of light appeared to be the major immediate impairment, but now he could see well enough to move forward.

Small limbs and the thick vegetation tore at him, but did not hinder his adamant resolve. Could he let God down now? Never, he thought. He stumbled, felt the sting of the thorns, and brushed at the countless limbs, but still he slowly moved forward. But to where, he did not know. He struggled.

A cottonmouth snake met his gaze. The snake's tongue slithered, but the animal remained still otherwise. Although there was present danger, the snake neither ran, nor attacked. It appeared to be in a trance, held in place.

Grant passed by hesitantly and did not turn to check the snake's position, but mentally thanked the Lord. Why this tedious journey and why alone? He wrestled with his mind.

That is a good question, a thought in his mind inquired. *Where are you going? It appears to me that you are just walking in circles. Didn't you just pass that tree minutes ago?*

Grant knew that the minions of doubt always attempted to cause discourse. They were the harbingers of doubt. When energized, they tormented their prey unmercifully. Grant was their intended and immediate victim.

Just turn around, go home. Ask your church for forgiveness. They love you. They will fall at your feet and worship you. You must hear them asking you to come home.

He would not engage these dubious thoughts. They were negative and would only hinder his travel. Brushing away new vegetation, he proceeded onward. He was amazed that he had not given in to exhaustion by now. As he cleared the thick field of trees, it opened into a small field of green grass. The sun's light shone bright and warmed him. A large apple tree with beautiful red apples stood in the center of the field. As he approached the tree, he remembered the garden of Eden and God's admonishment.

"Eat freely, this tree is for your nourishment." The sun's light appeared to speak to him. "Rest from your journey. There is more travel ahead." The voice faded.

Grant removed a large red apple and bit solidly. The succulent juices were sweet and pleasing. His thirst was abated. He sat and rested for a moment while he enjoyed the apples. The light he sought appeared before him at the bottom of a large range of mountains. The initial travel had lasted hours, but time and distance did not hinder Grant. He was tired, worn down by the walking, but still strong in his resolve. Where God led him, he would go. Grant fell unknowingly to sleep. The mountains, the high mountains of West Virginia, and he was asleep.

When Grant awoke, the tree was gone and the mountains were behind him. He looked around for the tree filled with those delicious apples, but it was nowhere in sight. He sought the mysterious light that led his way, but did not immediately see it. Like him, it had changed places. *Was it ever there?* he thought. Doubt gave life to his anxiety.

It was apparent that where he was now was not where he was before. A thought surfaced within him. *Who I am now is not the person I was before?*

A large river appeared to his front and the mountains to his rear. Had he turned? Was he still asleep? And are those deer to his side? What in the world had happened? Grant reluctantly walked toward the river's edge. The soft green grass seemed to provide him with a cushion for his aged feet. The deer looked his direction but continued to eat, then suddenly vaulted away.

Wondering when the deer would run, he asked himself where the guiding light was. He bent and cupped his hand, aware that he wanted a sip of water, which appeared cool and inviting. The water rustled against some rocks. Fish darted upward, splashing him with cool liquid.

Grant heard a noise behind him, which averted his attention away from the water. He turned to see a lovely lady standing behind him, appearing confused. He stood instantly.

"Hello," he said. He looked deeply into her eyes and saw nothing. They lacked emotion. It was if her stare was bottomless and was hidden beneath her soul, which appeared dull and lifeless.

She did not answer him, and he asked again, "Hello, how are you?"

"I crossed a bridge, but was driven away by a man with a flaming sword. Who I am, I cannot say because I don't remember where I came from."

Grant observed her closely and wondered, was she the reason he traveled in this direction…to find her? The light has gone. *Is this where it ends?* he asked himself.

"Sir, can you help me cross the bridge? I cannot cross it alone."

"Madam, what bridge?" he asked.

She pointed, "There." Now she asked him, "Don't you see it?" He looked over his shoulder, but saw nothing. "I am sorry, but

I do not see any bridge." He turned back toward her and saw the trickling of tears wetting her face.

She, with the soulless eyes that suddenly lacked life, brushed her eyes and spoke, "I think I am lost. I think I will never be found." "Travel with me, miss," said Grant. "I am also lost. Maybe we

will find our way together. My name is Grant." "I am Lena," she said.

"Well, pleased to meet you." He offered his hand. She was intriguing in appearance. Her eyes lacked life and appeared totally void of color. Her skin was velvety, along with her beautiful black hair. Only what apparently was a wedding dress that she wore gave her complexion contrast. She could have scared him with her sudden appearance, but everything was a bit irregular now anyway.

The river with its running water appeared to abate, giving Grant and his companion an easy way across. He turned and offered his newfound companion hope. He reached out his hand, which she took. He felt the cold lifeless hand that caused him to shiver, "Whoa!" he uttered repeatedly. Grant would not turn to look at her, but quickly traversed the river.

Caught up in the river crossing, he had not noticed that he did not have her hand any longer.

As he reached the river's other bank, he turned to help Lena. She stood on the opposite side of the bank peering across at him. "Lena," he said, "stay there, I will come back and get you."

"I don't think that you can cross back." She pointed behind him and began to walk away from the river's edge.

He turned toward the direction that Lena had pointed and saw the guiding light return.

CHAPTER 31

Jeb sat at the kitchen table, ingesting a piece of toast while sipping on a cup of black coffee he had hurriedly prepared. The house had a worn look, not the spectacular antebellum place that his dear wife had maintained. A day-old beard, nearly totally gray, graced his skin, which made him look older than he was.

It was nearly a month since she departed and went quietly in her sleep. He struggled at times with her death but assured himself that he would one day be with her in heaven.

His daughter, Mary, had returned to Washington, DC, following the funeral, which was attended by the entirety of Savannah's elite. They had overzealously attempted to comfort him, but lacked in their efforts.

Jeb thought of his daughter, often wondering how she would recover. He called her daily, or she called him. Their love made the loss less hurtful, but not totally reconciling.

The former pastor had abdicated his position and was now diligently working to help his former colleagues and churchgoers with the concept of brotherly love, a concept surely forgotten by the Christian community in Savannah, Georgia.

Many of the churches were populated along racial lines. Blacks attended black congregation churches, Whites attended white congregation churches, and the remaining city citizens did the same.

So heeding the admonishment from the man sent by God and who he now believed was sent by God, Pastor Lee tediously worked to establish a joined community between all the inhabitants of Savannah.

He was a diligent worker, suffering from the rebuttals, but standing strong against those that were comfortable with the status quo.

Many of his close friends attributed the change to the loss of his beloved wife, and persuading them that it was not the case was difficult. He labored countless hours to inform them of his total commitment to the brotherhood of men, and often fell on deaf ears. He had, in their eyes, changed, and his wife's death was a major contributing factor.

Recalling the conversation he had with his daughter following the funeral, she believed the death of her mother had profoundly affected him and this new pursuit precipitated from that. But regardless, she voiced her support.

One thing Jeb Lee observed was, individuals that lacked friendship with members of other ethnic communities more often accepted stereotypes. They more readily harbored deep-seated prejudices and unfounded suspicions. It was difficult for Jeb to unroot their false beliefs, making their transformation more difficult, while others sought change and challenged their inner self.

Jeb felt a bit reluctant to speak with pastors of other exclusive ethnic churches, but emboldened by a new inner peace, he challenged the pastors of the city to meet and exchange ideas and visit other churches regardless of the congregation's ethnicity.

Not seeing much change in his constituents, he remained adamant in his efforts to spread the good news. Spending long continuous hours, he was unsure if he had given enough.

There was a knock at Jeb's front door that relieved him of his inner thoughts and a long conversation with his mind. He subconsciously tugged his robe and tightened the belt around him. He had not had visitors in some time, and he was a bit excited that someone had come.

His gait reflected an old injury in his lower back. Numerous attempts by several physicians had not relieved him of the chronic pain. At best, the pain was temporary; at worst, the sciatic nerve sent electric shocks down his leg that several times felled him. He wished it would just go away.

Jeb grabbed the handle of the decorative door and opened it. With his mouth agape, he glared at his visitor, whom he had not seen in thirty days. He extended his hand without hesitation. His mind wondered why this man had come again. Had he failed his mission?

"Hello," he said.

"Hello, Pastor Lee," Paul replied, "and how are you?" "Just fine," replied Jeb. "Please, come in."

Paul made his way into the house, the same house that he had not been asked to enter during his previous visit. A more subdued person stood before him, obviously hurting from within.

Jeb offered, "Have a glass of tea. I was just pouring one for myself. Please excuse the house, I just cannot get this cleaning together. My wife did all of that."

"My apartment is atrocious," laughed Paul. "I used to have friends clean it for me, but now they don't stop by as often."

"Yes, there have been few visitors since I abdicated my pastoral position," Jeb unapologetically stated while alternating his seating position to ease the discomfort coming from his lower back.

Paul noticed Jeb's constant shifting around in the chair, but attributed it to him being there. "I will not stay long. As you recall, I gave you a message. A request. Those messages were given to me from the light angel. I have another message." Paul examined his host's face. "Your time on earth is ending."

Jeb wondered if he had done what had been enough and nervously adjusted in his chair from side to side. *What would this next announcement be, damnation or salvation?* he wondered. He believed that the last encounter was in fact real and that he had acted out of fear and had not relied on his faith. Faith would have freed him, but his heart was darkened by hate, a hate embedded deep in his soul and influenced by his surroundings. The subtlety of evil was so small and insidious that it slowly overcame reason.

It was exceedingly difficult to erase the bigotry of the times, which passed as pride. As he looked at Paul, he thought, had he ever hosted a nonwhite person in his home? There were the laborers, but never anyone he called a friend. Had he been the man of hate? Had love of mankind eluded him?

"Sir, I don't know why you have returned this day. I recall our last meeting. It did not end so well."

Paul was uncertain if Jeb Lee understood him fully, so he repeated, "Your time has ended here on earth." Jeb did not answer.

Paul continued, "I am your brother and not any different than you. Call me Paul, please. And you have assumed correctly, my friend. Your time has ended, and it is time that you join your wife. God is love and he has been well pleased with your efforts. The abrasive attacks upon you, the loss of your friends…your efforts have been appreciated. God loves you, be at peace."

Jeb's eyes filled with tears, and those tears slowly fell from his eyes. He wiped at the corners of his eyes, brushing the water away. A deep sorrow overcame him, and he began to cry, and emotions overwhelmed him. Jeb was uncertain of his future. He had worked diligently at correcting flaws in his life, the shortcomings that harmed others knowingly or unknowingly. "Sir…sorry," he said, remembering that his guest sought him to be more familiar with him, "Paul, have I done enough?"

Paul wondered how the emotions secreted in the life of this pastor now flowed freely and were unhindered, free to relieve the overwhelming grief that tenaciously held him. Held him so tightly that he was totally blinded and convinced that for all his life, people were different. Truth had freed him, and drained from within down his face.

"Sorry," he apologized, motioning toward his person. A heavy weight had been lifted from deep within.

"No need to apologize," assured Paul, who was attempting to console him.

Jeb continued, "Here is a great conundrum, rich people will never understand the souls of the poor people, regardless how philanthropic they are. The poor…both white and colored people, never understand the philanthropic. I am not so wise to offer anyone any advice that I have no knowledge. People must find within themselves salvation, a salvation that allows cleanliness. Any man could argue a point, but only truth is all-knowing. I read recently that in truth and spirit, we shall worship God. I now try to predicate my life on that fact."

Paul said, "I felt that feeling recently, that God is truth and spirit. I have said that before. However, I truly believe it."

Jeb added, "Yes, I need to apologize to all those people, sorry... people of color, that I have unknowingly hated all my life. Wow!" He shook his head and his body swayed. "Am I destined for heaven?" he asked.

"In truth, I don't know," Paul uttered. "None of that matters now. What you have done is done." He arose from his seat and placed his glass on the table.

"Sir, if I have offended you, I am sorry, please stay a while. It has been some time since I have spoken to company."

"Your journey is over, in this plane of understanding. God is calling you home, my brother. It will soon be time for you to join your wife."

"Have you seen my wife?" Hair rose on his neck. "Have you seen her?" Jeb asked. Jeb had become extremely anxious, causing his heart to flutter. Not wanting to offend Paul, and not fully grasping the totality of what had been said, the former pastor reached to grasp Paul. He did not want to be alone as grief welled from within.

Paul intercepted the seeking hands and held them lightly and eased Jeb back toward his chair. "Well done, I have been instructed to relay to you." Paul nodded.

Paul had not seen Jeb's wife since she called the police on him in Savannah, but he felt that all would be better soon for Jeb. A brilliant light opened a passageway toward the sky. It appeared to soar endlessly upward. Wings flowed downward and gave the appearance of white doves descending.

Slowly stepping away from the light, Paul prepared to return home. He had not witnessed this process, but knew it would be reassuring for Pastor Lee.

The pastor, with his robe pulled tightly around him, attempted to stand again, but the excitement of seeing the light surrounding him caused him to stumble backward, nearly falling. He reached for his chair to interrupt the fall. Startled beyond belief, he attempted to call to Paul, but could not utter the words.

A cloud slowly rose behind Paul, who had taken this journey numerous times before. *What was it that he was missing? he thought. I am certain that the dead had journeyed this way countless times before, but why am I here this time?*

An angel filled with light and welcoming hands reached out to Jeb, who had slumped back onto his chair. His body, with head lowered and hands hanging freely alongside, rested. However, a glorified body arose slowly with a hand seeking out the heavenly host. Jeb, his face brightly illuminated with a huge smile, grasped the hand of the angel and was lifted into the funneled light. A light with a brilliant glow and an uncountable number of angelic hosts were passing upward and downward. Jeb looked toward Paul, who returned a smile.

Jeb realized he was on his journey home and ascended quickly upward. Soon Paul's image had faded and the presence of his Jean, his dearly beloved wife, appeared.

What is this place? Is it heaven? he wondered, as Jean rushed toward him with her arms flung wide open. Jeb returned the hug, and he kissed Jean while hundreds of others soon joined the meeting and greeting.

Paul watched the light lift and fade and wondered, would he make the journey to heaven one day? The body of Jeb lay slumped in the chair, lifeless. Although he had just died, his skin had lost the luster and his appearance resembled a wax figure. Someone would find him here and offer several reasons for his death. Remorse, grief, and loneliness would be at the forefront. They had no idea.

The white translucent cloud began to swirl and overlap itself. It invited Paul. Paul's work was finished here, and his mind drifted to his initial meeting with Pastor Lee. He just stepped into the cloud and was whisked away.

CHAPTER 32

Fred unlocked the door of their newly purchased vehicle, then opened the passenger door for his wife, Jiri Maynard. Their children, Tracie and Maurice, sleepily stood beside them and jumped into their new SUV. The kids flopped onto their seats and secured their seat belts.

Assured that the children would resume their sleep, they headed away from Baltimore.

As Fred drove, he recalled his disturbing dream. He and Jiri had awakened suddenly from a deep sleep and stared at one other, ruffling the covers while sitting up in their bed.

"Jiri, I had a dream about a man sent by God, and he was admonishing me to take my family away immediately. It was strange indeed." He paused.

"Before you go further, I had a similar strange dream." Jiri was suddenly frightened.

Wanting to tell his story, Fred interrupted his wife, "There was a man surrounded by light, kind of like a glow. He spoke to me telling me he had been sent by God to give me a message that I should immediately obey." Perspiration visited his brow, which he instinctively wiped away. "He continued by telling me to gather my family, take nothing but the clothes they were wearing, and leave immediately. He said that I should not take any time to call anyone." Fred stopped and looked at Jiri.

Jiri responded, "I had the same dream."

They both moved quickly from the bed and went to awaken their children. No hesitation. Fred gathered breakfast cakes and fruit drinks, and placed them in a large brown bag. *Was there going to be a catastrophic weather event or an imminent war?* His mind was fully alert, carrying on countless conversations with no answers. One thing was clear, *leave this place now.*

Jiri roused the kids, who sheepishly were difficult to dress. She struggled to fully gather their undivided attention, but she never strayed from the task. "Hurry, Tracie, and help your brother, Maurice, get dressed." Jiri rambled, gathering her clothes. *Why such a hurry?* She fought away the doubt. *I believe.*

"Head west and travel to interstate 70/76 towards Ohio," instructed a voice, which overwhelmed his thoughts. Fred lived by faith, and he believed that he was given divine instructions. "I believe we are being commanded by God, Jiri. It is just a deep feeling that's burning inside." He teared up.

"I have trusted you all my life and will not doubt you now, honey," replied Jiri.

Fred replied, "What if this is a lie told by the Deceiver?" "Honey, it is by faith," she reminded him. "If this is the devil

that guides us, there will be no truth in it. If by God, faith guides us." Reflective, he found the support of her warm loving hand. Together they would travel this unknown path and would share the ending reward or distasteful fate. The car roared down the highway unabated.

CHAPTER 33

The sound of the intercontinental plane's engines roared loudly and drove the aircraft high into the evening sky. The sun glared brightly and extended for miles. Large white clouds filled the sky, appearing as floating pillows beckoning the heavenly bodies to lay their weary bodies upon them.

The passengers waited patiently for the all-clear sign so they could mingle about, gathering personal items to make their seven-hour flight more amiable. Window shutters were lowered at some seats, while being raised in others. Objects were stored in the overhead compartments, and other things were gathered.

An aroma filled the plane announcing the imminent arrival of nourishment. The flight attendants went about their work, preparing the meal and handling various inquiries from the many passengers. Many passengers looked for airline blankets, which offered them some warmth and made sleeping more enjoyable. Announcements echoed over the intercom, identifying the captain, who offered general information for the passengers. He assured them there were no weather issues and he wanted them to relax and leave the flying to him.

Valerie Romero sat in the aisle seat adjoining first class. She had plenty of room, and the seat was comfortable. Two other people occupied the adjacent seats in row 15. Valerie adjusted her seat and offered a warm smile and spoke, "Hi, I am Valerie."

Sister Rose returned a profound warm smile and offered her hand. "Hello," she replied.

The more loquacious of the three, as they would find out momentarily, Aisha, spoke, "Hey, y'all, don't forget me."

They greeted each other, discussed where they had been, and they had received a strange dream beckoning them to journey to Kentucky. All aspects of their recollections were the same, and these three travelers were moving by faith alone.

CHAPTER 34

Sweat eased onto his brow, which he swiped away without thought. Sheriff John Pickney, still humbled by the sting and hurt of the sudden departure of Pastor Longstreet. John felt so betrayed by Grant's deceit because he had loved him like a brother.

Emboldened by the brown liquor he was sipping, he contemplated how he could gather an appropriate revenge. *Years wasted helping this old fool who played me like a lovesick puppet. Somehow, somewhere, there will be a reckoning, and I will be the instrument.*

I can help you, my son, a silky whisper spoke in his receptive ear. *Whatever you need, I can assist you. You must stop the self-pity.*

Pickney heard a knock at his front door. He wondered who it might be since everyone in town knew him and would announce their coming by telephone. Although he was well liked by the inhabitants, it was never assumed their familiarity allowed them to visit the sheriff without announcement. He lowered his alcohol-filled glass to the table and reduced the volume on the TV with his companion, a television remote.

Occasionally, in exceedingly rare circumstances, a known acquaintance would stop by unannounced, but rarely.

He slowly approached the door and opened it. "Hello," he said.

His alcohol-drenched mouth oozed the recognizable smell.

"Hello, sir," the stranger replied with a wide smile. He continued, "I'm hoping to find John Pickney."

"I am he," replied John. "How may I help you?"

"Sir, my name is Al Lost, and I sell life insurance. It is a whole life policy that allows the owner to access any portion of the policy at any time."

John wanted to know more and invited the stranger in, directing him to his dining room table, where he frequently carried out his meetings with friends. "Now, if I heard you correctly, any money in the policy can be claimed at any time."

"That is exactly what I said. Any money in the policy can be accessed at any time," offered Al.

The sheriff said, "As you know, I am the sheriff, and this is a very violent job, so before we continue, what does it cover and in what situations?"

"The policy covers any manner of death…accidental, suicide, line of duty, and any other manner of death," replied Al.

"This appears too good to be true." Now more attentive, he uttered what he had been thinking, "And how much is this going to cost?"

"Well, it is a long-proven approach. You pay what you can afford monthly. As you become more invested, the payment slowly declines, and as a sign of good faith, the benefactor receives the dividends accumulated on the policy as payment. Basically, a no-lose life insurance. If you are wondering why everyone does not have this policy, it is because the benefactor personally scrutinizes all of the clients and offers this policy to those deserving."

"I wonder why he choose me?" inquired John.

"He found you through thorough research by his employees and wanted to give you something. He understands the requirement of law enforcement officers," replied Al. "Don't rush into the details of the policy. I'll leave these documents with you, and when you are ready, just call this number, 804-555-6666, and welcome in advance." Al rose from the table, shook hands with John, and headed to the door.

John asked, "Where is your office?"

"We are everywhere. The benefactor has a central location, which is accessible to all. Oh, by the way, where can I find Mr. Grant Longstreet?"

Anger immediately simmered. "That charlatan left weeks ago. I don't know where he is. If I can offer some advice, I believe he is a lost cause, destined for infamy."

Al smiled. "I did not know he had left. I was informed you were good friends," stated Al.

"That was right," responded John. Al smiled and departed.

CHAPTER 35

Grant cautiously approached a gnarly row of trees whose leafless branches intertwined. They were tangled together so tightly that it appeared as if it were dusk rather than midmorning. The sun's light fought for relevance in this unlighted path. The air was heavy and the moisture so dense it was like a sauna.

This was unnatural, thought Grant, but the glistening light shining in the distance had guided him thus far. He had followed the light this far by faith, and he would continue now.

Eyes from the woods followed him, and there were many. Nothing engaged him, and the only sounds that were prevalent were from his nervous feet clamping down on the forest floor.

Grant fixed his eyes forward, and his gaze was held by the beckoning light. Sweat slid down his back and rested on his pants. It was a steady flow of sweat, which agonized him. But that was a minor issue compared to the dungeon he was traversing.

Why this and why now? he thought.

The distant light grew wider now, and the trees began to normalize. Gone were the scary gnarly ones. Oaks and pines, even green grass surrounded him. He stopped and turned, but the scary forest was nowhere. *Am I dreaming? Who knows?* he thought.

There were no longer soaring mountains that kissed the low-flying clouds. Even the trees reached higher than the mountain peaks. Grant, whose eyes remained looking in the direction of the inviting light, trekked on without hindrance. This appeared as an over-whelming obstacle as he began his journey with earth's decorations standing before him like an impenetrable task.

Now the ground appeared flatter and his forward vision unimpeded. There appeared to be a gaggle of people milling around in the distance. As he neared them, he wondered why they had gathered in this field.

A familiar angelic voice came to him. The soothing sound was a voice that eased his soul. He was suddenly very tired, and his movement was greatly slowed. He could move no further, and he eased himself onto the fledgling greening grass. Sleep overcame Grant.

The bright glow that emanated from the soothing voice gained a physical shape and stood before him. "Let the peace of God be upon you. Give God the praise. You have completed your initial task. Well done. Before you are part of the elect which will join you, and you shall lead them forward." The ephemeral being swayed and continued, "Now the great movement begins."

Grant had many questions and wanted more details of what he was doing and where he was going.

The angel motioned him to silence. "Listen, your questions will be answered soon. When questions arise, rely on your faith, and if your questions deem an answer, it will be revealed. You must prepare for your journey. The people before you are here by their faith, but they are leaderless. You shall lead them. They all will not be led. For your and my adversary, who is now fully aware of your movement, will attempt to derail it before it starts. Many believe and many have doubts. They will be a hurtful thorn in your side. They will tempt the most ardent believer, and even their faith shall be tested. Stay firm and deal with the dissidence with your leadership, which has been honed over many years. This journey for you has been planned before you were born. Fulfill this mission, and God will welcome you home with open arms."

"Holy one, how will I lead these believers? They will not listen to me. When we face setbacks, how will I maintain my control over them?" asked Grant. He doubted that he could. "When they have questions and I have no answers, what will I tell them?"

The angel stared at him, his eyes filled with holy fire. "Did God bring you here where you are now? Did God place his arms around you and bring you here without harm? Why do you now ponder about these trivial things? God will give you guidance and will fill your mind with the words and actions you need. It was by your faith that you were chosen. Why do you now doubt? You must only believe."

Doubting his ability to accomplish God's plan was an insipid reminder that his professed faith and love for God and his kingdom was wanting. Grant wanted to awaken but lacked the ability to do so. "Those people gathered there are waiting for your leadership, your guidance. They have come here by faith alone. Look, they cannot all speak the same language, but they are trying. You must lead them. Fred will be your assistant and his faith is strong. Call for him and he will come when you gather with them. The Holy Spirit will flow over them, and their being shall change. They will speak to each other without difficulty, and they will have a strong urge to follow your leadership. The Holy Spirit has changed them, and they shall journey forward," voiced the angel.

"Your faith must be adamant. You must not waiver, because even now the minions of hell are gathering. They will corrupt the most faithful, making your journey more difficult. Some among you will receive the blasphemous suggestions and fall prey to the demons of the Beast's mighty army. Some of the select will even challenge the authority of God. They will be unaware of the unholy assault and will succumb to the wiles of the deceivers. Look around. These abominations from hell are arriving. They're gathering.

"I shall awake you momentarily. Have the select go and give their precious possessions away. Give their money, their jewelry." He hesitated and continued. "They are passed away, for today they are truly born anew. Go now and follow my directions. Do not worry over small things, for at the end all will receive a great reward guaranteed by God. Remain here for seven days, waiting for the rest of the followers. When your guiding light appears, begin your journey. Now awaken and be about God's work," spoke the mighty, soothing voice of the servant of the Highest.

Grant recalled vividly the words given to him, as he slowly stood. The matted grass below him assured him that he had lain there. He looked around searching for evil that he felt was whispering to him. *Get behind me, Satan,* he whispered in his mind.

Grant continued toward his flock as a sudden breeze washed his skin. He yawned, breathing deeply within. The air was like an invigorating elixir. His body felt the renewing strength. His age did not appear to be a hindrance. The long walk had laid his afflictions low.

Fred Maynard sat on the back cargo area of his vehicle under the raised rear gate. He watched his wife and children along with mothers and other children gather in a circle, arbitrarily assigning a person to run around the circle, touch another person who tried to catch the person who touched him. He could not recall the game's name, but recollected the fun he had playing the same games many years earlier. Screaming and laughing filled the air, and the participants appeared to be having the time of their lives.

He observed one child attempting to talk to another child who could only raise his arms and shrug his shoulders, a universal sign that he did not understand. They continued to laugh and pranced away.

His family, safe and happy, was all that he needed. The gathering had increased to over two hundred people since he arrived. He recalled arriving in this vacant field, arriving nearly simultaneously with three ladies stacking their suitcases at a single spot. The car they arrived in pulled away.

As the gathering increased, great variations in age, race, attire, and languages made him uniquely aware that great things were taking root. But why? He thought. How was he selected?

Looking to his side, he noticed a single person emerging from a long line of trees that extended for a distance. What was odd was that nearly everyone had arrived from the dirt country road in a vehicle. He glanced around to ascertain if others had seen the lone figure approach. If they had, they had not given this person an extended look.

Grant noticed more clearly now the diversity among the group, as well as their number, which was slowly increasing from the people in his original sighting. The game played by the children and some mothers paused upon noticing the arrival of Grant. The group gathered in a semicircle, diverting their attention toward the new arrival. It was something they knew to do.

If speaking to a gathered group of people appeared awkward, he felt the full mysticism of it now. "My fellow Christians gathered here, my name is Grant Longstreet, a servant sent here by God," Grant began, assuming everyone gathered was a Christian.

Those unfamiliar with the English language looked around, attempting to assess what was said and to what purpose. Those who spoke multiple languages were attempting to translate what had been said to those not understanding English.

Aware that nothing could begin until all the gathered could understand each other, Grant bent his knees onto the soft turf and began to pray. The gathering followed.

As Grant began to pray, many in the gathering heard, "In nomine patris et filii et spiritus sancti."

Others in the gathering heard, "En el nombre del Padre Hijo y Espiritu Santo."

And as Grant prayed, his words were being translated into the various languages of the world, and all who were gathered understood the prayer's meaning. Grant finished his brief prayer, "In namen Gottes beten wir."

A breeze swept through those who had gathered by only faith to an urging. It filled them with an indescribable sensation. As they rose from their knees, smiles covered their tear-drenched faces. Whatever was said was understood clearly by all. They all understood and spoke in one common language.

Demons moaned in agony as the power of the Holy Spirit conflagrated out of existence those demons that had ventured too close to begin their unholy assault on the gathered. Their request to their masters had gone unanswered. Their fervor resulted in an early final judgment by God.

A blue pickup truck sped down the dusty road, casting a cloud of dust from either side of the vehicle. It abruptly stopped, briefly skidding. Two men vacated the vehicle and rapidly approached the gathering, which now numbered about three hundred. Each approaching face held a menacing scowl. The elder man spoke loudly, "Who is responsible for this gathering?"

The owner, Jim Simmons, and his son, Harold, had worked tediously to maintain control of his property, but their efforts appeared to not be enough to temper the bank that held the loan. The government had not provided the support they had promised, which left the farmers in the area vulnerable to imminent bankruptcy. But being a proud man, Jim would not roll over and leave his land to the bank. He would fight to the end. Had the bank taken a preemptive strike, sending an investor to survey the land? His anger swelled.

"I am," answered Grant.

Not allowing him to continue, Jim Simmons spoke, "This is my land, and I want you to immediately vacate my property." His fist tightened.

"Sir, God has given me guidance that I should remain here as his servants gather, and after seven days we will leave," replied Grant. "There shall gather servants of the Highest. You will know them by their manner. A great light shall rise over them. Their truth is also your truth."

Jim had been restless the previous night, and a bright glow delivered him a message which he said had been sent to him by God. This message surfaced in his thoughts. *They will be from the many tribes of the earth, young and old.* "Are you Grant Longstreet?" Jim asked.

"Yes, sir," replied Grant.

Jim was now far more civil, scanning the crowd, whose every eye was examining him. Warm smiles appeared to soothe his harshness, his defenses diminished. *How does a dream reveal future events?* he thought. This dream held truths Jim could not comprehend.

"I had a dream last night that announced your arrival," said Jim. "Earlier in the evening similar thoughts revealed themselves, carrying a similar message. I did not give it much thought at the time. However, the dream appeared to support it. The dream was so vivid that it appeared real. Now to my surprise, it was truly real."

"I have been listening to voices in my head for the past months. I believe I have a feeling of what you have been through," Grant added.

They embraced. Grant and Jim smiled and walked away from the crowd. Harold followed behind, thinking of a date he had with his girlfriend that evening.

"How can I assist you while you are here?" Jim asked. "Your understanding is all that we need," replied Grant. "Food and water, anything?" inquired Jim.

"I have been instructed to ask for nothing, nor take anything from anyone, and other than the temporary loan of your land, we will not interrupt your life further," replied Grant.

Grant and Jim parted ways following their goodbyes, and Grant stated he would visit with him before he and his gathering planned to leave, which he knew would be soon. Grant felt an urging to separate from the gathering and made his way away from everyone.

Laughing and unintelligible talking slowly became distant as he returned to the area where he had first witnessed the group of people days earlier, and thoughts in his mind encouraged him to sit and rest. Nothing startled him any longer.

Grant slipped off to sleep, although to him it appeared as if he was wide awake. His mind was vivid, and a great light being appeared before him. The being, an angel that was familiar to Grant, approached him, while Grant lowered his head.

"Give glory to God," spoke the angel.

The voice of the angel spoke softly into his mind. It was as if he could hear and understand every word exactly as it was given. *On the morning of the seventh day, you will depart and follow the guiding light. You shall have the gathering carry nothing, no jewelry, no electronics, no personal items, for all shall be made available for the faithful. Those that are injured, need medicine, and the maimed shall have no need of assistance. The Lord God shall remove all calamities. They will experience a new birth free of things that bind men's souls. Some shall want to retain personal items but assure them that these items are and will be of no use. The things that bind men must be lost so that they are free. Beware that those who are gathered are not all children of the Highest, for among this gathering are the deceivers, the unclean, the defilers of the Word. They shall be a deep thorn in your side and will work vehemently to deter you, but have no fear as the Lord has guided you here, so shall he guide you to his appointed place for you and your following. Be of good cheer. He shall not forsake you. These are the commandments of God. Speak with the people and make them aware of what will be required of them, and at the end of this trek, they shall be truly rewarded.*

Time appeared to have passed slowly for Grant, as he felt the angel in his presence. After the final instructions were received, he could not grasp how long he had been asleep because things that surrounded him had not changed an iota.

Before Grant could return to the group, Paul Lawrence emerged from the trees. He approached Grant and offered his hand, which Grant received. "Paul?" said a startled Grant.

"I am here only to assure you these dreams you are having are real. The messages that you have received as you know or assume are angels sent to you by God. I am the physical manifestations of them. A human messenger to affirm their reality."

"Will you travel with us?" asked Grant.

"No, sir, but whenever you need assurances, I will come to you," replied Paul. "I have traveled and still travel at God's command. Mostly assuring people what they have heard, dreamed of, or that new missions are real. Many of the people that are gathered here have seen me."

"Do you know what is going to eventually happen to this gathering of people?" inquired Grant.

"No, I do not," replied Paul. Paul eased away, waved to Grant, and returned to the row of trees.

Grant composed himself and returned to the gathering. His first action was to find Fred Maynard and speak with him concerning the commandments of God. Fred was informed that he would be Grant's second in charge and would hand out the discipline to those that had violated the commandments of God.

"Gather the followers into a large group and inform them that I shall advise them of our departure and their personal requirements. Have them gather en masse. Pass the baskets of large circular brown wheat bread, the bottles of water, and the baskets with an abundance of colorful fruits to them. This shall be their evening meal."

"Do we have enough to feed the multitude?" questioned Maynard.

Grant's only reply was, "God will provide." He had given his entire life to fulfill whatever role was required of him. There would be no doubt in him. "Please, if you see Rabbi Moshen Levi, ask him to see me following my speech to the gathering."

Rabbi Moshen Levi was a younger man, much younger than Grant or Fred Maynard, but very learned in biblical studies and religious studies. He had taught for several years at a prestigious university and had done years of religious historical research. He had been recently working on US government research grants to authenticate ancient discoveries. But now he was a follower of Grant, drawn to the group by an unknown insatiable desire for knowledge.

After hearing Grant's universal television conference, he had written to Grant, but had not received any response. A great urge overcame him to join Grant in Kentucky, and upon his arrival, he was funneled into the site where the group had assembled.

CHAPTER 36

As the multitude gathered, rounding into a circle and partaking of the food, which was in abundance, Grant thought of the guidance which he received, and wondered, was he the right man for this mission? He fought inwardly with the anxiety that was more real than not. His palms began to sweat, and his heartbeat rose incrementally. "Where are you all going when you leave from here?" asked Jim.

Compassionately, Grant answered, "I don't truthfully know." His hands movement directed his response, "I simply follow the directions given to me, and most of the instructions just suddenly come and suddenly go. Dreams most often convey the information."

Jim recalled his dream.

"There is a small favor that I must ask," Grant said coaxingly. Jovially, Jim replied, "Ask away."

"The gathering's cars, the jewelry, the possessions we cannot keep. Some have brought their total savings, over millions of dollars. Will you take them and use it for however you see fit?" asked Grant. "I cannot do that. That is a lot of items to just leave behind.

Why don't you sell it if you cannot take it with you?" queried Jim. "My instructions were to take nothing with us but the clothes

that we wear. Nothing else matters, and this material wealth shall be given to someone identified as fulfilling God's command. It has been revealed to me, that one is you," Grant spoke confidingly.

Jim Simmons stood flabbergasted. His once demanding demeanor had eased, and now he felt embarrassed. He was indeed embarrassed even in his thoughts. *How could I have been so confrontational? The unknown is ever the antagonist, often without validation, but always challenging.* "Why give it to me?"

Grant saw the hesitance in his newfound host. "Jim, please be assured this is part of a mysterious plan which I have no plausible answers. For whatever reason, this is where I was supposed to be at this certain time and place. How we are relevant in God's plan, I am just not totally certain. But God has directed me to pass the wealth of the gathered people to you and he said it would help you. So here we are."

"Maybe my family and I can join you. If God is directing this, this is where I should be and where I should be joining with you."

"Listen, whatever the plan is, your part of the plan is to be here," encouraged the pastor.

Grant began to speak. His voice carried to the crowd as though he was standing beside them. "We will be leaving this place the day after tomorrow. We shall travel as a group as God leads. We shall not separate into small pockets of people that resemble each other, are of the same racial stock, or of gender or ethical designations. Do not worry for when you communicate with others, they will hear and understand you fully. We, as Christians, have forever loved with hate and hated with love. This journey shall be a gathering of Christians journeying into the unknown guided by faith. The young, old, and infirm shall travel without unnecessary assistance. We shall know true love when the journey ends."

He looked over the crowd, not gazing at anyone in particular, and continued, "Leave all your belongings, jewelry, funds, devices. There is no need for vehicles. Mr. Simmons, our local host, shall take control of these items and prepare for when he is called to perform God's works." There was grumbling from the crowd. Some faded and some increased. Some had much wealth and their wealth had controlled their desires. Grant noticed that it stirred the people. "And again," he continued, "where we are destined, I have no idea why and what our destination is. I have no idea. You have all been called by him, the Highest, and he expects by faith you shall travel. For those that wish to leave, it will be your decision, your free will. Take your belongings and leave."

Grant waited and watched the mass of people make decisions, some departing while some stayed. Grant would not interfere as he watched hundreds depart. The gathering regrouped into a smaller pocket.

He continued, "Please leave your valuables in the pickup trucks with truck beds. Love that you will be loved. Remember the commandments: Love your God with all your hearts and mind and love your neighbors as yourself. Do not covet, do not lust, do not steal. We shall face many challenges. The minions of the devil shall assault us every day, but he shall not prevail. Give him no room to hover.

"Do not worry about your clothing or what you shall eat, for all things will be provided that you will need to survive. Fred Maynard and others will be available to you to inquire about your concerns. As I end, gather your clothing that you consider you will need. Gather blankets and devices to drink water. You will need nothing further." Someone shouted, "Only one drinking cup for each family member? Any changeable cloths? What about medications which I

must use daily?"

Feeling anger rise within him, Grant settled himself and spoke. "There is no need for your medicines, your anxieties, nor your reservations. All you need will be provided to you. Most importantly, bring your faith."

"There are lovers of the same sex, prostitutes, and sexual deviants among us," another called out.

Grant only replied, "Judge not. Just be accountable for your actions."

Standing now in silence, the group began to disassemble and seek places to settle for the night. It had been a long journey for many and a tedious trip for others, but now it had culminated in this greening field of soft grass whose exact location many had no idea.

"Pastor Longstreet," a soft voice spoke.

"Yes," Grant answered. A tall but small-framed man stood before him. He was nervous and transferred his weight side to side.

"Pastor Longstreet, do you really accept everyone to this gathering?" he asked.

Pastor Longstreet looked into the eyes of the young man, seeking any clue to this sudden meeting. He had mingled freely among the gathered people and had afforded to all an audience with him. There was no need for an appointment. "Son, it is not I that have sought anyone in particular to this group. I will cast no one away."

"My partner and I came to this place. It was my insistence that he drove me here. However, he has left. I am alone, and the many unwelcoming stares and whispers are making me wonder if I should also have left."

"Young man," said Pastor Longstreet compassionately, "everyone here has been invited and many have departed. Everyone came from an inward urging and some have left because of the unknown. I can understand their fears. As I have said, all are welcomed. What is your name?" inquired Pastor Longstreet.

"Edward Miller," the man replied.

"Then, Edward Miller, walk along with me during this journey. Let us travel together as friends, and if any scorn you, I am also scorned. Take good care that our fates are equally bound. Any that hate you, also hate me."

A few of the group that were always near Pastor Longstreet looked at the two men. They gave no outward response, but whispered in silence among themselves.

CHAPTER 37

"See you guys when you get back," spoke Paul. His best friends had just dropped him off in front of the hospital where he worked.

Rebecca held tightly to Paul, who wanted to move backward. Although she was one of his best friends, the intimacy of her hug made him uncomfortable. She giggled, knowing that hugging people unfurled hidden anxieties. "Not so fast, joker." She giggled. "Give me a firm, emotional hug."

"Leave him alone, Becca, leave him alone," joked Daniel. He shook Paul's hand, firmly nodded, and moved to the driver's side of his car.

"Bye," added Rebecca, assuming the front seat next to Daniel. "Keep my cat fed, please," she added, pulling the door shut but encountering resistance due to the seat belt handle being caught in the door.

Looking through the car's window, Paul admonished Rebecca, "Keep my boy safe!"

Unknown faces moved in and out of the hospital door, indifferent to their surroundings. Patients, visitors, and employees, all comfortable in their own unique situations. Many, but not all, were always victims of spiritual warfare with an insidious unseen challenger who clandestinely sought out souls for the great manipulator. Paul was glad that Rebecca would be accompanying Daniel to Chicago. They were his best friends and always attempting to manipulate his life; however, they would help him in any way. Paul was happy that he would not be left alone with Rebecca, who always harbored plans within plans, plans to provide joy in his life.

Paul had stepped onto a slowly grinding escalator that vehemently fought the mechanical gears while roaring its disapproval. He adjusted papers in his hand while his stomach challenged his mind. He had not eaten breakfast, and his stomach craved satisfaction.

Favorite of God, a familiar voice whispered in his mind. A voice quite familiar to Paul. *There in the cafeteria is a young woman who is lamenting the death of her father. She is at a crossroad, uncertain of her future, which has caused great turmoil in her life. She is at the verge of abandoning her faith, a faith that was always at the forefront of her life. Go to her and give her assurances of what you know and have seen.*

How will I know her, angel? he mentally responded.

You will know her. Hell's minions have found her and wish to devour her. Look for the darkness. There she can be found, responded the angel.

As suddenly as he rose, in the mind of Paul, his thoughts had rapidly faded away and resurfaced. Paul thought, *If I would try and explain what goes on in my mind, they would confine me in a mental institution for sure.*

People milled around inside the hospital cafeteria. Small conversation among coworkers and visitors alike kept a riveting humming in the large room. Since it was lunchtime, there were quite a few people placing meal orders and many more awaiting their time to place their orders. Paul thought of how many times this daily event had occurred.

Metal chairs screeched across the tile, growling aloud time after time. It bothered some, while others so familiar with the noise gave it no attention. Dishes scraped the tables, adding to the inner workings of the cafeteria. Paul wondered how many times these events had repeated themselves.

I am looking for someone and how quickly have I forgotten my tasking, he thought. He moved to a clear area of the room to scan the cafeteria. Straight ahead, to the sides of the room, and basically simply looking around, searching for his assignment among the horde of people.

Leave her alone, she is mine. It will be awfully bad for you to interfere with a prize of my lord. Always dystopian, the minions clamored incessantly, often boasting over nonevents. The many voices bombarded

Paul's mind to such an extent that he wanted to cry out, *Just leave me alone!*

That is not going to happen, the voices in his mind continued. *If you, in any way, interfere with our work, you will suffer dearly,* hissed the devilish minion.

Get away from me, his thoughts engaged with these tormentors. "In the name of Jesus, get behind me, Satan!" cried Paul.

The command had driven the demons hurriedly away, and now Paul's fragile mind returned to task. A darkness hovered around the cafeteria, but a deeper darkness, like a moving shadow, gathered around a specific table whose lone inhabitant was a single girl. It was odd that many people were searching for seats, but all avoided the table occupied by one lonely inhabitant.

He stood with his mouth agape, looking into the face of someone he knew, at least he had met her before. Her head was bowed, her eyes heavy, swollen with tears. "Mary?" Paul was asking with a bit of uncertain recognition.

"Hi," Mary replied, holding back more tears.

"What is the matter?" he asked while sliding the legs of the chair backward. "Is there anything that I can help you with?" he inquired. "No," she replied. "I just had some emotions that came to surface."

"They must have been very profound personal thoughts," said Paul.

"Well, both of my parents have died within the last month. My dad just recently passed in Savannah, Georgia. They were always so supporting and gave me the most wonderful life."

"Were the deaths expected, or did they just come suddenly?" Paul thought, *Why have I asked that question?*

She looked toward Paul with her blue eyes centered in reddened sclera. "My mother died in her sleep, which was not expected, and my dad died at home in his chair. He was a preacher for all my life, but following the death of my mother, he had abdicated his preaching ministry and had begun to teach on the totality of all believers, Christians.

He seemed to be renewed in his beliefs and changed his teaching efforts to loving thousands, neighbors, no matter their situation."

Paul replied, "I wish I had met such a person."

Mary looked at Paul and said, "In his certain way, he was a very great person."

"Is there anything that I can do?" inquired Paul. "Not really, but thanks for asking," she said.

Mary stared at Paul, and without conscious thought, she said, "I was in such a melancholy state, I was actually contemplating suicide." Paul felt a powerful jolt deep inside his soul, feeling his mind seeking answers to questions now emerging. He looked at Mary more

directly. "May I ask a question of a personal nature?"

Mary, bowing her head ever so slowly, acknowledged his request. "Please speak freely."

"I don't know what Rebecca and Daniel have told you about me, but God has granted me some insight into his immediate plans concerning the plight of men." He stopped, not knowing why he was explaining this.

The active cafeteria with the many patrons seemingly became louder. It was as if the volume was being orchestrated by others. Paul was not naive and was cognizant of the efforts of the unholy to thwart the efforts of the Highest.

Emotions were overcoming him, and whispers in his mind shouted, *Tell her!*

"They have only said good-willed things about you. They both love you to death," she said.

"Well, good, I have known them for an exceptionally long time, they are close to me. I have known Daniel since high school, and he is as close as a brother to me."

"So, who are you?" she asked.

"Just a normal guy who has been given certain gifts that allow me to carry out God's Word. I was directed to come to the cafeteria to prevent a suicide, and as I entered the cafeteria, a certain darkness hovered over this table, so I deduced it was you."

Tears filled her eyes and rolled unabated down her face. She said, "What you have said is true. I was considering that. I just felt lost and had temporarily lost hope with the sudden death of my parents. It was as if I was…am, alone now."

"Well, I know you are not alone. If Rebecca calls you friend, you are never alone." He laughed.

"She is rather loquacious, and her humor is uncontained. But how do you know God?" she questioned.

"I'll tell you the redacted version," Paul stated. "I have been given an ability that allows me to move freely to wherever there are people who have been designated to fulfill God's plan. I then inform them on what they need to do, I am like a physical presence on earth for the heavenly world," he said.

Mary questioned him, "How am I in this plan, and why was I chosen?" Her eyes widened, although the redness from crying shaded her eyes with a tint of pink.

"I am not certain because I only recently received this mission. The thoughts just surface in my mind." He spoke apologetically, "Truthfully, I just do not know."

Tell her that God has need of her assistance and that she must travel to the Midwest to meet with Pastor Longstreet, tell her the events in the world, heavenly and unnatural, that require her presence and unknown to others that are gathered together, they are waiting for her arrival. She must take nothing with her, the familiar voice that appeared clearly in his mind whispered to him. Tell her that you were with her father when he died and assure her that he is with her mother in heaven awaiting her arrival. Tell her.

Paul knew that if he told her, she might cause an unavoidable situation. He worked with some of these people that were eating in the cafeteria, while others knew both of them.

She will not believe you, but you must tell her, whispered the voice. What appeared to be several moments, was actually less than microseconds. Paul believed, because he was given insight, but was always a bit hesitant when revealing God's directions. *Could these meetings be alone in some more comfortable situations?* Paul thought to himself.

"What role you are playing and why you must be there, I have no idea. But your presence is required. Soon you will journey with me to Texas, and there you will be given an assignment."

Mary gazed at him and exclaimed, "I am not going with you anywhere. This is absurd." She continued, "This so-called plan is bogus. What do you really want? Are you some sort of pervert?" She was becoming extremely angry.

Paul was once again unsettled when dealing with these events requiring explanation, but had only the information given to him.

"If you think that I am driving to Texas with you and leaving my belongings behind…are you some sort of a quack? I am not going to do that, and I am, matter of fact, going to go home right now," she said.

Tell her that you knew her parents and that you were with her father when he left his physical body and went home. Tell her.

Paul touched her hand as she was pushing away from the table. "I was with your father."

"You do not know my father!" she shouted aloud. "You did not know my father," she said. She glared at him; her eyes filled with consternation was stinging him, piercing his very soul. "Just leave me alone!"

Some of the many diners looked in the direction of the sudden raised voice that sounded louder than the converging sounds of the many voices. The turmoil of these days necessitated that the attention be directed. It gave reason to give pause.

"I was with your father when he ascended to heaven, and I watched his physical body slump back onto his favorite chair. As I am physically here and was directed to this table, I was given instructions to be with your dad before he died."

Some people had looked at the two people while others just simply ate their lunch. No one was startled enough to intervene.

Tell her what Charlotte Monroe's last words were when she departed this physical plane. She wanted to soothe the pain of her passing. She issued admonishment for those that did not know Jesus as their Lord and Savior.

She had a much greater concern than her death, spoke the voice that manifested in his mind.

"Listen," stated Paul, "a family friend's daughter, Charlotte, died as you entered her hospital room in Walter Reed Hospital, and her last words were that she loved you all."

Mary Louise was more startled at this revelation. She asked, "How do you know James Monroe?"

"I do not know who that is," he responded.

"The father of Charlotte," she replied. She stared sternly toward him.

"It was just a thought in my head that suggested that I mention it to you. There are greater forces working in and around us that want your immediate attention. Why you were selected for this, I cannot say that I know that, but you have been selected. Your father was given an opportunity, and he did not believe me either, but following the death of your mother, he believed. I believe because I have witnessed these events. You must believe now by the faith you have. Just like me, why you were selected I just don't know."

Mary slid the chair backward and stood. She gathered her belongings and turned to depart.

"Listen, you have but a short time to listen. The saints are gathering and they will depart very soon without you. If what I have told you does not give you pause, then leave, but if it does, heed it. Your soul may depend on your next moves."

Off Mary went while Paul stood looking and wondering. *I guess I was not convincing enough,* he thought. He watched her leave the cafeteria.

CHAPTER 38

You may become so fascinated with possession that you may become possessed yourself. Paul lay in his room and in silence on his worn leather sofa, which had been given to him by his dear friends. He searched for the TV remote but was displeased that he had to stand to retrieve it once he located it. He was the ultimate procrastinator when there was no dire need to achieve. *Where did that admonishment come from?* he thought.

Allow me to get back to what I really enjoy, and that is, doing nothing, he thought. No missions, no angels, no assignments. He was trying to relax, but he lived with a nervous anxiety, which lingered with him lately. *I really want to get that TV remote and see what is funny in the TV world.* Easing from his seat, he slipped to his knees and made the short crawl to where the remote sat. He laughed. *That was not that bad, but when are lazy actions a chore? Now let me see what I can find.* He pressed the power button.

The large screen TV appeared to come alive. It began to evolve into human form, dark lovely forms. They appeared to be attempting to tantalize him with salacious shimmering, lustful mannerisms, and lude mental suggestions. They were whispering sensual thoughts in his mind.

Lovely Lena appeared, prancing seductively across the room, which had its light dimmed, while similar images materialized in his presence.

Just seek me, the voice sassed.

Forgetting his admonishments to never engage with unnatural things, Paul asked, "Where are you? How can I find you?"

The false image now began to stabilize in his presence and soon assumed the image of his lovely Lena. She appeared to gently kiss his cheek. Her tongue eased across his face.

"My love, you have returned to me. I will never leave you again," said Paul.

"Yes, my dear, I believe you, but you must do this one thing," she said.

"And what is that?" he asked. His mind dwelled on her image, which was stored in fissures in his mind.

But you are not willing to do what I ask? questioned the voice.

"Anything to be with you, my love," he replied.

"Then come and join me." She beckoned while moving away from him. "Come and join me," she said.

Paul stood and walked toward his lovely Lena. He appeared entranced as he stumbled forward. His hands sought her grasp.

As she slid toward him and whispered in his ear, "Denounce the Holy Ghost and we shall forever be as one." Her teeth nibbled on his ear.

Paul began to speak, "I d—"

A sudden flare of light burst into the room and materialized. The image of Lena erupted into flames and hissed as it returned to the immaterial realm.

v There was no inflection in the angel's voice, just a bit of disbelief.

Having stumbled away, attempting to avoid the light, Paul had stumbled and fallen. He pushed himself to his knees, then stood. "Sorry," he replied. More than anything, he wanted Lena to return. It was lonely without her.

CHAPTER 39

Mary Louise was in a mind-challenging fog. Affected by the meeting in the cafeteria, she sought closure and wondered why Paul knew so much about her and her family. She gathered her purse, checked her face, and headed out of her building. She decided to walk the short distance to where Paul stayed. She had visited with his close friends, Daniel and Rebecca, and had been to Paul's apartment once. She held her cell phone, debating if she should call Rebecca to alert Paul she was coming over, but decided against it.

Suddenly startled, she noticed a man prone on the ground, his body lay on the grass while his feet dangled on the sidewalk. People leaving other buildings and some just walking the street stepped onto the roadway or stepped over him to avoid contact.

The man, attired in worn clothes, lay silent with blood oozing from his forehead, his hair matted, and his eyes lacking luster. It was difficult to know if he was even living from her vantage point. She approached the fallen man cautiously, and bent alongside of him. His breathing was shallow, and his face had lost the luster of life. Pale and unconscious, he lay alone.

Several people glanced at her as they strolled past, some casting an inquisitive glance toward her. The contrast between the appearance of the two elicited more stares of bewilderment than concern toward the obviously injured man.

"Sir? Sir, can you hear me?" she asked. Mary repeated the question.

There was no response forthcoming. Recalling her CPR training, she was poised to take immediate action when she noticed that he breathed ever so lightly. Her cell phone in hand, she dialed 911.

An ambulance arrived within twenty minutes as she estimated, with roaring sirens and excitable lights. People appeared more attracted to the lights and noise than the man who appeared on the brink of dying. He had not moved, but Mary was assured that he was alive. His life signs, though faint, were present.

"How is he doing?" an excitable tech approaching Mary asked. "Alive, but unresponsive," she responded.

"Who is he?" the tech asked, bending alongside the man.

"I do not know," she replied. "I walked up on him." She paused. "And this is how he was. His situation has not changed since I have been here."

The other technician pushing a gurney approached. People began to walk by, casting sideways glances, emotionless and lacking empathy. Mary wondered whether they were even concerned. Probably not.

One tech spoke to the other after examining him, including rifling through his clothes. "He has no ID, let's take him to General Hospital. They will not be concerned about his condition nor his ability to pay."

"Take him to Metro Central Hospital. I'll cover the cost," stated Mary.

"Do you know him?" inquired the tech. "No," she replied.

"Then, our protocol is to take him to General Hospital," replied the tech.

Mary called the operator at Metro Central Hospital. After being transferred to the financial office, she explained what was transpiring and provided the finance manager with her credit card information. She gave permission to use whatever funds that were necessary to treat the unknown man, who would be soon arriving by ambulance in the emergency room. She informed the finance manager she had more funds should they be needed.

Being inquisitive, the person in the financial office asked why she was being so generous to someone she claimed she did not know. "I have the means to assist him financially and elected to do

so, and what does it matter how I choose to spend my money?" she responded politely. Her Christian values emerged from within. *Love thy neighbor as I love myself. He is my neighbor.*

"Then, what is his name?" the finance manager inquired.

"I call him a Child of God, that is good enough for me. Can they transport him now?" she inquired.

"Let me speak with the ambulance attendant," the finance manager directed.

He accepted the cell phone from Mary. "Hey! Transport the injured man to Metro Central, his bill will be covered and use my name as directing this movement."

The tech returned Mary's cell phone to her, and without further questioning, he placed the gurney into the vehicle and sped away. Mary continued toward Paul's apartment.

While slowing her gait, she needed answers and emotional stability before speaking to Paul.

The apartment complex was secured by an attendant, along with a security officer. They scrutinized each arrival, questioning their business, and all visitors needed a resident's name to access the complex. The officers would then contact the resident, and after acknowledgment, would direct the visitor to the elevator and release the elevator. All visitors were viewed by visual monitors while in the elevator and followed to the apartment on the monitor.

Mary Louise fumbled with things that she secured in her pockets, keys and several coins, which had not made their journey into her handbag. The elevator was ordinary, nothing to tantalize the eyes. Mary's thought was on the imminent meeting with Paul, an acquaintance, not necessarily a friend or even friendly. Memories surfaced vividly, illuminating thoughts that had urged her to this meeting.

Paul had tossed clothes in his room, filled the sink with dirty dishes, and folded a calico blanket that he used more often than the blankets that covered his bed. He was cognizant that she would eventually visit with him, but had not anticipated the suddenness of her arrival. He moved unencumbered about like a busy bee attempting to tidy up his small abode.

A knock startled him; it echoed loud against the silence. He made the several steps to the door, which he opened. Before him stood Mary Louise, the daughter of the preacher that he had watched ascend to heaven. The friend of his dearest friends stood before him like some impish child. Her rosy cheeks highlighted her sparkling eyes that were welcoming. He could not see the nervousness and shyness within. "Come in, but please excuse the apartment."

Mary stepped inside, quietly and quickly scanning the apartment, which was adorned with many pictures, some framed, some simply tacked onto the walls. They covered nearly every square inch of the apartment. She had never been alone in a male's apartment and was understandably slightly nervous. She had been to Paul's apartment before with Rebecca.

Paul readily saw the nervousness encompassing her and began to gather humorous thoughts in his mind that might ease this awkward encounter. "It takes a while to clear the clutter, which gathers equally as fast. I never can figure out how that happens."

"It is not that untidy," responded Mary Louise, standing inside Paul's apartment.

"I try to do better each time," he responded. "But lately I have been in and out," Paul added.

Mary Louise refrained from looking directly at Paul and stood in the middle of the room, while Paul eased behind her and shut the door. He stepped back and offered her a seat on his couch, which he offered to everyone while seating himself in the lone chair that sat directly across. There was a transparent glass table that separated the couch and chair.

Mary Louise, her eyes rambling, broke the uneasiness. "Paul, have you heard from Daniel or Rebecca?"

A bit surprised, he responded in the negative. There had been only an extremely rare occasion that he had not spoken to Daniel daily, and several days without contact was rare indeed. "No, I have not. They must be enjoying themselves in Chicago," Paul responded.

Mary looked around the apartment, searching for conversation pieces. Her upbringing held her lips closed.

Without announcement, a great light manifested itself in the room, its brilliance glowing, then materializing into a physical being. "Fear not, Mary Louise, I have been sent to you by God, the Highest. He has need of your services."

Paul recalled his initial meeting with the angel, and while watching Mary Louise, wondered, had he appeared equally frightened?

Mary Louise pushed hard against the sofa, trying hard not to cry out. These were strange days, and strange was the happening within this apartment, strange indeed.

"I have come with good tidings from the Lord, and bids me to give you his peace. He is with you even until the end of time," spoke God's servant.

Paul only watched and listened, wondering how he would find his way into this meeting. What part would he play? He knew from the past that somehow his involvement was certain.

Mary Louise only looked in disbelief. Her mind was quick, and she recalled how Paul's story concerning her dad's ascension into heaven did not seem so far-fetched now.

The angel then began to speak of his mission. "I have been sent to you to explain God's mission for you. Time draws near, and the fulfillment of his will shall not be hindered."

"There is a man, Angel Concepcion, that is being detained at Fort Sam Houston, Texas, along with his family. This man had been directed by God to meet Pastor Longstreet before he arrives in Iowa. While proceeding, he was detained and imprisoned at the military installation. While heading to Kansas, the authorities gathered him under their control and placed him in prison. While in prison, he has gathered a following who have come to accept God's justification and faith. The Great Deceiver has spewed lies and innuendos among the flock, and now their faith has begun to waiver."

Mary Louise thought she might be dreaming and wanted to speak, but her mind and lips were not coordinated, and while she appeared to want to ask a question, her thoughts were confused. Tears welled in her eyes.

"I have confused your mind, and you must listen now," spoke the angel.

The angel continued, "Even as I speak, the devil harvests souls of the faithful, so you must hurry. Bring Mr. Concepcion with you, and together you shall travel to Kansas and meet with Pastor Grant Longstreet. Those that remain faithful will be reunited with Concepcion in time, but their time is not yet. He may bring his wife and daughter with him, but that is all. As the devil gathers his minions together, they will challenge your every action, but stay strong."

"Why was I selected?" asked Mary Louise.

"God's will is his alone. I only bear his will," spoke the angel while he faded away.

Mary Louise looked at Paul in disbelief and was searching for his confirmation of what had transpired. "What just happened?" she asked.

"We must go, Mary Louise," Paul calmly spoke.

"I cannot leave yet, there are things I must do. Think about this, I cannot just pick up and leave," she said.

Paul responded, "We must leave now." "Are you going?" she questioned.

"I will escort you there, but this is your calling," said Paul. "I am not going. I refuse," she said.

Paul knew this exchange was not heading anywhere, and without further conversation, the mist gathered and encompassed both him and Mary. He knew that everything happened as God willed it. She could speak with God later and have her questions answered. He had seen enough to believe, and she would also soon know what he knew.

A white cloud enveloped both of them, and within moments, they stood on the roadway leading into the military installation. *When would this dream end?* she thought. She sought out Paul for support, but he was nowhere to be found.

Mary was obviously overwhelmed as she looked around, searching for some landmark that would identify her whereabouts. She noticed a large structure to her front that was secured by what appeared to be military personnel. She felt the humid heat that caused her to breathe more deeply. Beads of perspiration found form on her face.

The short distance to the gate entrance was just that, short. She walked across the grass while cars approached the gate's entrance. Each vehicle was met by uniformed personnel and directed forward.

For some reason, she did not see how she was going to just pass by the officers at the gate. Nervously, she approached the security officer, searching her mind while anticipating what she would say.

"Ma'am, may I help you?" a tall slender security officer with a broad smile asked.

"Yes, I would like to enter the base," she replied. "May I see your identification, please?"

She had only now realized that her purse remained in Paul's apartment. "I have left it at home," she replied.

"Sorry, ma'am. Without any identification, I cannot allow you to enter," he said.

"Sir, I need to visit a gentleman that is residing on the installation," she stated.

"Without identification, you cannot enter," he politely responded. "Is there a telephone number that you can use to contact your party?" he asked again while becoming more alert. He reflectively began to scan her person, searching for any irregularities.

Mary Louise had no idea what she was going to do or how she was going to return to Virginia. Walking slowly away from the gate and to nowhere, she sought answers to questions that assaulted her consciousness in waves. Although seconds had passed, the onslaught overwhelmed her mind.

Why have I come here, and I have no way to return? she thought.

I am with you always, responded a comforting voice.

Mary Louise strolled along the road entering the base, and turned the corner. The roaring sounds of many vehicles went rambling by.

Got to find a bank and get some money. Her survival instincts were returning her mind back to normal. Her fears abated. *Which way should I go?* she thought.

As she slowly continued walking and now realizing the blistering heat would task her with additional concerns, she knew she would have to slow her mind or lose total control. A horny frog sped across her feet and stopped. She hopped backward. *Glad it was not a snake,* she thought, watching the horny frog scurry away.

To her amazement, the tiny frog passed around a tree that appeared out of place. As she followed the movement of the small critter, she noticed a large opening in the fence that was hidden by the tree. The frog stopped and looked back at her, seemingly bidding her to follow.

She contemplated her next actions, but not for long. She entered the installation, scanning her surroundings for sentinels that she believed would soon be upon her. They never came.

"Where to now?" she murmured aloud.

CHAPTER 40

Pastor Longstreet had awakened early in the morning just as the sun's light began to make its presence known. It parted the darkness with ease. Grant could hear life around him. Crickets and birds called to each other while a doe and her fawn loped before him.

Another journey into the unknown. But this was different. He was not alone, he thought. The robe he wore draped around him to contend with the morning's coolness slipped to the ground as he stood.

"Praise the Living God! Let his will be done, and if I can play any part in it, let it be. Your faithful servant always." He whispered aloud, "Let it be."

It was not long before the light overcame the dark and set the day's things into motion. People began milling around gathering their meager belongings and anticipating the day's events. Little children, oblivious to the upcoming events, searched around for new friends and whatever activities they could become involved in that resulted in playful joy. Watchful parents gazed upon them with eagle eyes while still gathering their few belongings.

It was not long before everyone in the group was stirring about, wondering, *What now?* There was reservation about what was going to transpire. They had uprooted their lives, and by faith they had come. Inwardly, the unknown fueled their trepidation.

No one noticed where or when the refreshments had come. There were baskets filled with fruit, bread, pastries, cheese, and an abundance of various food and plenty of water. Some of the adventurous and innovators mixed juices and lemons along with honey to create familiar morning's sustenance.

Grant, along with Fred Maynard, overlooked the crowd and discussed the upcoming events, of which they had limited information. They were soon joined by Rabbi Levi and Jim Simmons and his son, Harold.

Grant asked that they pray for the pending sojourn into the unknown. Regardless of where it led or how long it took, Grant knew that he would never doubt his mission. While praying, he opened his eyes and viewed his selected companions. They were traveling on faith alone, and something must have urged them forward. That something had to have been the same Holy One that had spoken with him.

He spoke aloud, "My Lord God, my Messiah, my Redeemer, please give us the confidence and guidance to complete this task. Where you lead, we shall follow without complaint and without personal concern. We acknowledge that you remain with us always and shall remain with us until the end. In Jesus's name, we pray." His eyes reddened as water welled in his eyes. His eyes burned.

"Rabbi Levi, gather with the lead elements of our group, be their eyes and ears, their sounding board. I don't believe this journey will go without an enormous assault from our great enemy. He will prey upon the weak and those that are mentally infirm. There are many that have faith, but need assurances."

Moshen nodded and headed to his position.

Without guidance, Fred proceeded toward the rear of the gathering while smiling as his family joined with him.

Grant vigorously shook Jim's hand and hugged him heartily. "Jim, take what is left, and I hope everything goes well. We appreciate the borrowing of your land and the unsolicited sharing of your gifts."

Jim and Harold made their way toward their truck. He had much to gather and itemize. There was much wealth to assemble and catalog before it could be transferred to financial gain. He watched with deep affection while Grant moved toward the front of the assembled group.

He somehow became profoundly moved by this gentleman, whom he only recently met.

Grant led the group as they began to follow, many wondering where they were headed. But by faith they followed.

They had gone only a few feet before their initial challenge came to fruition. An ominous cloud, dark and vicious, with high violent winds began to expand and shield the sky's light. It roared loudly, and it rained with such intensity that its forces knocked many to the ground. Some of the group ran from the darkness, heading to their previously owned conveyances. They were lost before they had begun.

Grant stood firm like a stone wall, praying to his God, his protector, his champion. "The devil seeks to destroy our solidarity before it begins, give us comfort against these principalities and unholy minions. None but you can stand against this evil without fear."

You have been given charge over those assembled, a whisper spoke in Grant's head. *Cast these evil things aside. Evil does not have the power to harm you.*

"In the name of the Mighty Protector, our Lord, get behind me, Satan!"

Grant spoke this powerful phrase and watched as the light rays pierced the darkness. The winds abated, and the rain ended as quickly as it had started. Grant scanned the gathered and was pleased that they had stayed together against this unscrupulous threat, although not totally satisfied. He was saddened as he observed those that had scurried away. They were wandering around without direction. Their lack of faith had cast them aside. They had been admonished against the devil's wiles. What more could he have done? His inability to confide assurances had caused the loss of several members even before this journey had begun.

There was no sign of the tumult that had passed. The land was dry, and the wind subsided. It was if it was just a baseless memory, but in reality, it was much more than that.

The gathering followed the direction of Fred and Moshen, and began their journey. Kids were playing as they walked, and the elderly moved along with the others, void of any previous impediments that had hindered them, some for many years.

Alone at the head was Grant, now imbued with holy power. There were no hindrances. His gait was smooth and natural, and his stride gave no indication of his age. His eyes were clear, and the light before him shone bright like a lustrous beacon.

The devil had called his champion to his side. "How is the plan proceeding?" he asked, his voice penetrating the fabric of his servant. "It proceeds as planned, great one. They will fail their God,"

replied the servant. "None can stand firm against you," he assured. "Your platitudes will not save you if you fail me, I can assure

you," spoke Satan. "You will be kin to those that incessantly burn and are tormented. Fail me at your own peril!" The devil stared deep into the mind of his acolyte. His words burned within.

"Master, I will not fail. Even now I gather those together that will destroy the plan of the false god. I have gathered the seeds of the total destruction of the great plan. You will remain as the great emperor, the true king of kings," he hissed.

The devil vanished with no acknowledgment or confidence in his servant. He left a parting message, "Don't fail me!"

CHAPTER 41

The Great Deceiver, arrayed in his brilliance, held audience with his uncountable minions. They snarled, hissed, and praised his unholy presence. "All, listen," he spoke. "A time is nearing, and it is soon upon the world when we have an opportunity to lay waste to God's plans." More growls and cries of consternation interrupted him. He continued, waving for quietness. "I have been assured that God's plans are being subtly unraveled as I speak. People have been placed in strategic positions to end these plans."

The great demon glanced around with a look that made his entourage shudder profoundly within their souls.

"These"—he pointed toward his laborers—"our existence relies upon their efforts," he snarled as his many forms swirled in and out. "They have assured me that God's plans will be permanently interrupted, and thus, the infallible will now become fallible. Their existence is at stake. In my kingdom, there is no room for failures. Some that eternally are tormented shall rise and assume a new station should my directions fail. They shall replace these tormentors and feel the depths of eternal torment."

Frightened, millions remained silent as they pondered his last statement. That the tormentors would become the tormented.

The Great Liar faded away, bringing with him the implementors of his desires. They dared not speak, but rather rendered great praise upon their master.

CHAPTER 42

Daniel and Rebecca passed the tedious time of driving by listening to Rebecca's incessant talking, which was indeed endless. She was overcome with being on the road with her husband, and she was spellbound by the wonders of nature. Tall trees, gigantic mountains, endless roadway. Top it off, she was with the love of her life, and alone with him.

She talked, and the miles marched rapidly by. There was no need for any other entertainment because she was entertainment enough. Happy and free.

Daniel loved her dearly and for the most part always engaged her with similar stories of his past, or created stories that complemented her interest and her love of intrigue, which she found in everything. He thought that this trip would replace the deep hurt of losing her dear friend, Lena, which was held in abeyance by her boundless activity.

When she was not talking or listening, she was counting the car types, their manufacturers, or simply their colors. It was exciting, and she enjoyed it.

A loud pop and the suddenness of their vehicle's movement careening from the roadway caused Rebecca to scream aloud, while simultaneously reaching for Daniel, who was fighting for control of the great iron horse. The vehicle ripped through the guardrails as though the metal was paper and gave no resistance. Gravel flew freely, splattering the road and grass like automatic machine gun trajectories.

Daniel fought with all he had to avoid free falling over the embankment, which would bring certain injuries or death. He thought life could not end this way. He felt the tugging of Rebecca clinging to him, and then the free fall. Her hands let go of Daniel and flailed about, unconsciously reaching to the car's ceiling, attempting to brace herself. It would soon be over.

Time flew by silently and just as quickly as the landscape they had driven past earlier, without the slightest concern. Daniel wondered how death's cold grip would overcome him, and how it would accompany him to take him home. If there was a consolation, his dear wife would be joining him.

Daniel and Rebecca, this fall does not have to claim your souls. There is a way that all of this can be averted, a soothing voice engulfed their minds. *Relax, relax, things will slow down.* As if the voice was a fortune-teller, the rapid fall crept to an immediate standstill. *See, it is as I have told you,* continued the voice. The fall stopped.

Daniel and Rebecca now faced another image, a well-dressed man, debonair and confident. His eyes appeared without emotion, and his gentle smile was pleasant. "All things are possible with a certain faith. Believe deeply with your soul, and life's burden will pass uneventful."

Daniel inquired, "What is going on?"

"You have driven off the road and are falling to the bottom of this ravine," answered the visitor.

Rebecca looked in wonderment, trying desperately to find answers. There was no rational reason they had not crashed to the bottom.

"My benefactor has need of you and wanted me to explain that to you. He has a favor that he seeks from you, for a favor in return. After some repairs you, and your spouse shall be on that long-awaited journey together," he spoke very calmly.

"What do you want?" asked Daniel.

"Not I. My benefactor," he spoke. "But first, I must ask you a small favor," said the new arrival.

"What?" cried Daniel. He wondered why he and Rebecca appeared to be suspended in the air.

"You must say that you denounce the Holy Spirit and that you will pledge fidelity to my benefactor."

"Is that all? Is this a dream? Who is this Holy Spirit that you speak of, stranger?" Without waiting for answers to his questions, he assumed responsibility for Rebecca. "We denounce the Holy Spirit!" thundered Daniel.

"No! You must both say it," ordered their visitor. Rebecca said, "I renounce the Holy Spirit."

Daniel replied in kind, "I denounce the Holy Spirit."

"I will visit with you in the future and your favor shall be due." The strange man faded as suddenly as he came.

The car rambled roughly against the ravine floor without breaking apart, and slowed rapidly. Daniel grabbed the steering wheel and rode the vehicle to rest.

"Are you all right, Becca?" asked Daniel.

"Yeah," she responded, while inhaling deeply. Her heart pounded in her chest. She grasped Daniel's hand for comfort.

"What happened?" asked Daniel.

"We fell over that cliff and somehow rested here unharmed," she responded.

They looked at each other, wondering what had just happened and thought about what they had done. The otherwise loquacious Rebecca sat in silence. There were no imminent answers, no solid explanations, nor why they were still breathing.

Several people who had observed the vehicle falling from the road came running. They slid cautiously down the rocky embankment, taking care not to fall face-first. They approached the stopped vehicle. To their amazement, two people sat seemingly uninjured. No one gave it a second thought as they afforded the vehicle's inhabitants with caring assistance.

Daniel and Rebecca exited the vehicle uninjured and thanked everyone that had come to their assistance. They were now full of smiles and handshakes. They wondered, had this fortune been real or had they slipped into purgatory or some other phantom dimension?

Daniel wondered inwardly how they were to get back onto the highway from where they had landed. Unbelievably, there was a dirt road that appeared to circle around the cliff from which they had fallen. But was that for sure? he thought.

A burly man spoke, "This dirt road travels around that mound and spirals upward to the highway. If you all are okay and there appears to be no damage to the vehicle, just get on your way. I think someone called an ambulance and the police. Maybe it would be better to just wait until they arrive."

Daniel did not know how long they would be delayed but reconsidered just leaving the scene of the accident. As far as he could see, nothing was damaged and no one was hurt. But leaving the scene might be misconstrued. Excitedly, he informed the crowd while simultaneously alerting Rebecca that they would be there for a while. The screaming of sirens answered his thoughts. They would be delayed. But explaining what happened would be a different matter.

CHAPTER 43

Al Lost and John Pickney sat at the diner and ate breakfast, exchanging small talk. Pickney occasionally spoke to fellow patrons who spoke as they passed in and around the small diner. An occasional smile from a patron across the room caught his eye, which he followed with a nod and smile.

Al Lost just picked at his food, which John noticed. "Aren't you hungry?" John asked, before biting a crisp piece of that delicious Virginia bacon.

Al nodded, but directed a question at Pickney. "Have you heard from Pastor Longstreet or has anyone in town spoken with him?" He was certain that the relationship had been severed, but needed confirmation.

"No one that I know, and I have not heard from him," responded Pickney.

"Well, my friend," spoke Al, "I have some knowledge that I received from some of my acquaintances, and they believe that he might be in Kentucky. They think he has joined a cult or another false religious gathering."

"You don't say," answered Pickney, while rubbing the grease from the bacon onto a napkin.

"Yes," responded Al.

John was far from interested. He had known Grant a long time but had not spoken with him since John had been enjoying the lavish life that money had given him. He remodeled his home, purchased a handsome vehicle, and held lavish functions in the town. He was more popular than ever, and he adored it.

"Well, my benefactor has a certain interest in Grant, and he wants you to go to Kentucky and meet with him, and determine what he is doing and where is he going. He believes there are plenty new possible owners who may need some of that insurance money."

A bit hesitant, John wanted to refuse and said so, "There has to be plenty of others that he knows that will go there and obtain that information."

"Certainly, there are, but you are highly favored with my benefactor. The effort you put out in South Goering was awe-inspiring. Those people lavishing in decadence, self-love, godlessness, lovers of each other, and an unquenched desire for hedonism was disgusting. But not deterred, you refused to judge them and gave them hope while boldly offering the benefactor's insurance policies. After what I told him, he was overjoyed. He personally asked me to have you make the journey."

"You know I will have to get someone to take my place here for a while," John answered.

"The benefactor was plenty certain that you would have no problem finding a replacement. He has the utmost confidence in you. I should not say this." Al hesitated. His hesitation was for inference.

"What is it? Go on," requested John.

"My benefactor wishes that you join the organization and run this sector of the country. The pay will triple what you make, and will be less time-consuming," replied Al.

John Pickney was spellbound. Could he take up a new prestigious position at this time in his life? From what he had seen, it would be life changing. He pondered deeply.

Al Lost read the emotional state of John and snickered within. "Please don't mention this when he meets with you later in the week. Let him propose the offer, whether you accept it or not," he instructed John.

John released another piece of bacon onto his plate, wiped his fingers, and looked deep into the person of Al Lost. "You know I am a great actor." He giggled. "I will play this low key and accept the offer."

They enjoyed a laugh and shook hands. "Remember, don't lead on that you are cognizant of what he wants to say," Al reminded.

John spoke to himself with eyes aglow. *Now my true purpose is revealed. I always believed that I was more than just a sheriff. I will travel the world as a new man spreading the joy of this philanthropic man.*

"The benefactor wishes that I accompany you when you meet with Grant," said Al. "He wishes that you make our introduction."

John nodded. "The benefactor has been very gracious with me, and I will be more than honored to help him."

CHAPTER 44

After greeting the doorman and exchanging greetings, Rebecca and Daniel walked wearily down the hallway to their apartment. The drive had been long and tedious. The miles crept; over and over the scenes ran together.

Both entered their apartment and collapsed onto the sofa while pushing their luggage away with their feet. The comfort of home was welcoming and momentarily freed their minds of that near-fatal fall. The agreement they had jointly made with their benefactor luminated in their minds.

They wanted to discuss the event, but their reticence found no avenue for conversation, which was unusual because Rebecca loved discussion and nothing previous caused this desire to abate.

Daniel grasped Rebecca's hand and spoke, "What have we done, my love, and what price must we pay?"

Rebecca leaned toward Daniel and kissed him tenderly upon his cheek. "Whatever happens, I will never cease loving you, and nothing will ever change that," she said.

"And I love you," he replied.

"Should we call Paul and let him know that we have returned?" questioned Rebecca.

"Just a few minutes," responded Daniel. "I think things will soon change and somehow interrupt our lifelong friendship," said Daniel.

Rebecca added, "I don't believe anything can break that unbreakable bond. You two are closer than brothers."

"Yeah, it is just the unknown," he replied.

Rebecca said, "Call Paul and ask him if he wants to join us for dinner. Let's have Chinese."

"Paul. Rebecca…how have you been? We are back," spoke Rebecca.

"Hey, girl, how did you enjoy the trip?" asked Paul.

She responded, "It was exciting, and Chicago was really nice. The buildings, the food was delicious, even the people were not so bad."

"Hey, glad you guys enjoyed yourselves, but I am glad you are back. I missed your annoying voice." He laughed.

"Well, thanks, friend. The reason I called was to invite you to dinner." She flopped onto the couch. "We are ordering Chinese. Do you want the same, egg foo young with egg rolls?" Rebecca rested the phone against her cheek, simultaneously removing the dirty clothes from her suitcase.

"That will be fine," responded Paul. "Give me about thirty-five minutes or so."

"Great!" said Rebecca. "We will see you then," she said. "Okay, remember to get soy sauce," he replied.

Rebecca moved toward her husband and caressed him. She always felt secure when he was around. His smile, his love, everything about him charmed her. Even when they had a small spat, he would recall something humorous that eroded the discourse.

"Hey, what is that for, girl?" he replied jokingly.

"For nothing in particular other than expressing my love," she replied.

He brushed a small kiss on her forehead. "I love you."

She responded with a more passionate kiss and replied, "Not as much as I love you."

They looked at each other and appeared to ponder what they had done. It certainly was not good. Daniel spoke, "Let's confide in

Paul. Maybe he will have some insight into what we have done and how we can rectify this."

An eagerness overcame her, and she spoke, "He, better than us, should know."

Daniel replied, "Yeah, my man. He will be more so attuned to this supernatural stuff."

Rebecca, now more jovial, replied, "Certainly."

"That hero will be here soon. You better order that food," said Daniel.

Pulling her cell phone from off the table, she dialed the number, which she had saved in her phone. "Hello, I would like to order some food."

There was a knock at the door, which startled the two. There had been no announcements from security alerting them to a visitor, and they had just ended their call with their dear friend.

Paul would not have knocked on the door if he were expected. He would have just come in and flopped down on the couch, waiting patiently for his dear friends.

Daniel moved to the door with Rebecca closely behind. Their raised eyebrows silently questioned who it might be. Daniel approached the door cautiously even though he did not expect any issue. He positioned himself in a defensive stance with his left foot leading. He opened the door.

"Hello," the raspy voice uttered. "Your friend is here." Al Lost stood tall and intimidating. He was well groomed, wearing a suit that fit him perfectly. His sardonic smile was disconcerting.

"Well, invite me in, friends."

Slamming the door would be more inviting but was not the best thing to do, thought Daniel. "Sorry, please come in," said Daniel. Daniel offered his hand, but it was not received.

Al Lost walked in and scanned around the apartment. "Remarkably interesting," he said. He noted a large framed picture of Jesus hung centrally on the wall near the table. "I see you are hanging the graven image of God. Such a pity, the true god will not fault you, but I would prefer that you take him down."

Not sure what to do, Daniel gripped the hand of his first love tightly. "Sir, that is a gift from my dear, close friend. I cannot and will not remove it. He will be here soon, and I suspect he would wonder where his gift had been moved."

Rebecca, more verbose, remained reticent. She was beginning to shiver at the sight of this stranger. She had seen him before, and only once. It was under extreme circumstances. She had not recalled his being. She had not wanted to.

"Please take a seat," offered Daniel, while gesturing with his hand.

"I will not be here much longer, and my business here will be very short," replied Al. He sneered at the couple. "Your favor has come due," he responded with emphasis.

"What do you want?" replied Daniel, remembering the deal he had made with this man.

"A very small favor, and I will consider our agreement complete," spoke Al Lost.

"Okay, what is it?" asked Daniel. "How can we come to this resolution?"

"I have a favor, a personal favor, which involves your friend Paul. He has come to the attention of my master, and his actions need to be temporarily curtailed," spoke Al.

"I will do nothing that will hurt him," retorted Daniel. He looked directly into the eyes of Al Lost. "Nothing at all."

"It is often so unappreciated when one saves the life of a friend and he lacks the common decency to honor a pledge, albeit an unequivocal gesture. I have no intention on hurting your friend. I just want him to realize he has more to gain than to lose," spoke Al.

"What is it that you want, sir?" questioned Daniel.

"Security is about to call, letting you know that your Chinese food has arrived," stated Al. "Now whoever gets the food, don't alert Paul that I am here."

Rebecca was none too happy to vacate the apartment to gather the food. She wanted to alert Paul but was cognizant of the ominous admonishment. She did not want to leave Daniel alone. She did not wait for the elevator but hurriedly made her way down the stairs to the concierge desk.

Rebecca wanted to alert Paul, feeling their friendship was far greater than her safety, and that this malcontent person was at her apartment and desired to hurt her friend. She juggled the bags of food nervously in her hands. She ran to the stairway and swiftly made her way back to the apartment.

She arrived and noticed that Daniel and Al sat quietly in the living room. Had something happened? Everything looked all right, she thought. Paul had not arrived, so except for the two of them, nothing was happening that needed her intervention.

"The food is here," she said.

The silence in the room was so real; she felt it was palpable. She placed the bags on the table and looked at Daniel, hoping that he had the answers that she wanted to hear. "Honey?" she started.

"Sorry," said Daniel, "my thoughts were elsewhere."

Daniel avoided the cold, callous, hunting stare coming from across the room. He could never hurt the only real friend he ever had. They had grown up together, enjoying the good times and lamenting the worse. He longed for the quiet, joyful days when their parents were around, and they were so carefree that nothing caused them any prolonged grief.

I love that guy, he thought.

Al Lost commanded, "I need you to fulfill your promise now." "Soon, Paul will be knocking at your door. I need for you to welcome him as always. Overcome him with joyful greetings, hug him, relax him. He needs to consume this pill. Do not worry, it is not intended to harm him, but to put him to sleep." He watched them.

"He will sleep for several days, awaken, and not be any the wiser."

Al continued, while noticing their facial expressions, which were wide and searching for answers. "My word is my bond. It will not harm him in the least."

Daniel felt he could not trust this man. "What is in the pill?" he asked.

"Just an immensely powerful tranquilizer, you could get this over the counter at plenty pharmacies. Everyone has them," said Al.

"Watch." He placed several tablets in his mouth and swallowed them. He waited several minutes before speaking. "What did I tell you? It has no effect. I'll probably fall asleep soon, so I must be going. Good luck, my friends, hope to see you soon."

Al Lost turned away smiling and exited out the door. He leisurely walked down the hall before fading away. He was assured that his mission would be completed. "I'll see them soon."

CHAPTER 45

Paul was searching for the pair of his favorite tennis shoes, a black pair with white shoestrings. He fumbled over his clothes and other things that had found refuge in the corner. Tossing and searching items repeatedly did not disclose their location.

Maybe I'll wear my house slippers instead, it's just around the corner and a floor down, he thought.

Beware, an unsolicited thought entered his mind. But beware of what? he thought.

The pair of shoes that he was searching for stood beneath a set of piled clothes. "There you are," he said, smiling. "Now for some Chinese food. Keys, cell phone, diet Cokes, that's all."

He headed out of the door for a short walk to his friends' residence as his mind battled with the admonishment, Beware.

Daniel and Rebecca held hands, then embraced each other tightly. They could not abide by the request. A strange request from someone who appeared whenever or wherever he wished. And this pill. Would it harm their dearest friend in the world?

"Rebecca, I cannot consider placing this unknown substance in Paul's food. My life is worth nothing if it hurts Paul," said Daniel.

"I agree with you, dear. I would rather die if it would hurt him," said Rebecca. She held Daniel's hand more tightly. "I love him to death. Who knows how he became the object of this threat, or why would someone want to hurt him?"

"It was a glorious day when we met that man," said Daniel.

"Indeed," replied Rebecca, griping her husband and best friend more tightly.

Daniel grabbed the bottle of pills and removed the cap. He slowly funneled several pills into the hand of his dear Rebecca and several into his hands. He returned the bottle onto the cabinet surface. Watching, he saw tears erupt from the eyes of his loving spouse. "I don't know how this will end, but I would not change a single thing in my life. You and Paul have made life so wonderful. Each day was like living in paradise."

Now lost for words, which were being held in abeyance by powerful emotions, "I love you," she said, "even more today than when I first looked into your eyes."

Daniel held Rebecca close and tight enough to feel the pulse from her accelerating heartbeat. "Let us do this quickly. Paul will be here soon," said Daniel.

Without speaking further, they swallowed the instruments of their demise and made their way to the couch. They embraced and waited for whatever was seeking them. It came frighteningly rapid. The slow, insidious prickling fingers of death gripped them tightly.

The distance from Paul's apartment to his lifelong friends was traversed in seconds. Down the stairway and down the hall, he had repeated this trip numerous times and gave it no thought, but the burning in his legs always reminded him of his physical regression. He knocked and playfully repeated it by knocking several extra times. A sulfur smell eroded his consciousness. He was familiar with the offensive odor. It caused him to pause.

A turn of the doorknob excited his consciousness. What evil lies within? Entering the apartment, Paul immediately observed his dear friends asleep on the couch. "Wake up," he called. "Wake up." He rushed toward them, seeking signs of life, but found none.

The warmth of their bodies had not faded. "Wake up!" he cried. Paul fell to his knees while clutching his head within his hands. "Why?" he cried out.

Paul's angelic companion stood alert beside him. He was attentive to the ongoings. His strong hand gripped the hub of his powerful sword.

The small demonic imps who were now tormenting the souls of Daniel and Rebecca remained a great distance from this heavenly warrior. These spawns from hell tugged and gnashed at the hellbound souls. Their assault was unrelenting.

Paul fell hard on his knees and cried out, "My God, I just can't stand this any longer." He wept. Tears flowed unhindered and continuously down a natural valley along his face. "The more I do, the more I get punished." His head moved side to side.

Even his guardian felt his pain and wanted to express passionate words that might ease Paul's anguish, but he knew none. "God's will must be done."

Rise. The angel lowered his hand onto Paul's slumped shoulder. *God has heard your cry, and those that by their words were lost shall not feel the fire of the eternal pain until he decides on their judgment day. Your love for them has postponed a lifetime of despair. Come now, great demons long for your very soul.* The angel's emotionless gaze never retreated from the minions of hell. His inspiring glow filled the room and cast away all interlopers.

Having no more friends, Paul felt lost. His soul cried out loud, but no one comforted him. He regained his feet and flung himself onto the couch between both of his friends, pulling them closely to himself. Their warmth receded, and they appeared as mannequins in a store window. They never appeared to have ever been alive.

Call security from the hallway, he thought. *I have to get out of this apartment.*

CHAPTER 46

Rebecca and Daniel walked hand in hand down a narrowing road into a deep cavern. The acrid smell pierced their thoughts, bringing fear to the front of their individual minds. They experienced a gut-wrenching pain. It was constant and continuous.

Small, stinky servants of disgust prodded them along, shouting blasphemous curses at them while jabbing them with pointed burning steel. "Praise the beautiful one, praise him at all times, only he knows the truth," they repeated over and over while their demonic smiles surfaced as they leapt along.

"My pretties, he awaits, and he is not satisfied with you two," lambasted the snickering minions. "You are going to enjoy your new home. The price for betrayal. You humans are weak and lustful." Some tormenters were louder and more accusing, but all lacked compassion.

Rebecca felt burning claws scratch at her skin and heard the repeated torment. She wanted to scream, but her voice was silent. Her mind became the orifice for communication, but it found no recipients.

A familiar figure appeared in the distance. It did not appear welcoming. Curses oozed from his mouth, filled with vulgar obscenities. Daniel could see numerous smaller impish figures seeking recognition, skipping around him. Some scattered from his powerful strikes but returned immediately, avoiding his assaults.

Daniel and Rebecca knew they had reached their life's end and they would suffer deeply for their betrayal. Gaining some semblance of confidence, Daniel welcomed the idea that he had not forgotten his friend, Paul, in his hour of need.

Al Lost spoke to his betrayers. "So you felt that you did not have to return my gift? Well, you shall for the rest of your life feel the torment, torment of despair. You shall long for peace, but you shall never again know peace. These servants will torment you continuously to infinity."

Small minions erupted into a snickering laughter. As they laughed, the nasal-assaulting sulfuric fumes oozed out.

A brilliant light flashed, with bright lightning bolts erupting around Rebecca and Daniel. Ten great angelic beings emerged, clad in light-emanating armor. They positioned themselves in front of Rebecca and Daniel. The tormenting demonic minions fell away, running frantically behind the great demon Al Lost.

Temporarily startled, the great demon was forced back, held away by the great flame-doused swords of the angels. He called out to countless succubi and fiends. But they too were held in place by the brilliance of the angels.

The great demon bellowed out curses against his opponents. He offered assault with his great sword, but it was easily parried away.

"God demands these souls! Interfere and meet your fate before time appointed," spoke the angelic commander.

"You have no control here," spoke the great demon, emboldened by his many cohorts.

The angels increased their burning brilliance, which forced the demons. "Away, foul fiends," spoke the angel. He directed his pointing finger in the direction of the great demon. They could not contend against the Champion of God.

The angelic host departed the depths of hell, along with Rebecca's and Daniel's tainted souls. They settled on the side of the nonjudged and released Rebecca and Daniel, then departed.

Rebecca and Daniel looked around and immediately noticed a bridge, which appeared as a gateway. Emerging was the person of Lena, who looked at them with a blank smile. She was not elated to see her friends because she knew that their existence on earth had ended with them wanting. But otherwise, she thought it was good seeing them.

A large angelic being stood tall with a sword of fire guarding the bridge, separating the saved from the nonjudged.

CHAPTER 47

With head lowered and his eyes swollen by the erupting tears, Paul made his way to his apartment. *Again and again the resolving truth repeats itself, you shall not know lasting friendship or love. Attach yourself at your own peril and await the folly and torment that shall follow. It certainly will.*

But with Daniel, their friendship had survived against onslaughts from both sides when white and black people lived in different worlds. There certainly could never have been any closer bond than the one they shared, and whatever transpired here, somehow Paul knew this calamity was to save him from harm. He opened his door and fell upon his couch. The anguish fell upon him once more. His head, filled with emotions, sought relief. He simply gave in and wailed loudly.

Along with several of his acolytes, the great deceiver wondered aloud, "When God's host contends with impunity in the realm of my lord, there must be retribution against these interlopers. Gather my army, and we shall together challenge this false god on his turf. I want the soul of God's minion. That should please Satan, and he will look at me with greater respect, give me more command responsibilities," he snarled.

Acolytes channeled in, "Great one, you are highly favored, the highest. Give us command and we shall carry your will. You are the greatest among us." In repetition, they continued their boasting.

The great deceiver's enormous feature straightened. *Do they think that I could challenge Satan for command of our abode?* A smirk caused his lips to rise.

Satan entered his thoughts. *Overstep your position, fool, and you will see how the tormented live! Fail me again,* the whisper carried a forceful admonishment with it and deep pain.

"Master, I never would attempt to usurp your authority." The demon lowered his gaze and kicked away those that were exalting him. "We have work to do," he challenged.

CHAPTER 48

Valerie, Rose, and Aisha walked unincumbered through the fields of green grass that was their walkway. Where it led, they were equally unconcerned. Aisha kept them entertained with her boundless quantity of stories, many she created on the spot, but occasionally reliving her life in these colorful narrative accounts. Her gift of anecdotal recollection was transfixing.

Her two companions always listened attentively, always amazed at the clarity of her storytelling and tranquil recitation.

They had driven from New York together after vacating the plane that traveled from Europe. Being driven from within by some unknown desire to travel to Kentucky, a place they had never previously considered, the three followed their inner desires that propelled them.

Now in their two weeks of travel, each day was more fulfilling, sauntering along to wherever this journey took them. "Hey, look," said Aisha, ending her story in midsentence. "Fred, how is life treating you today?" Aisha spoke.

"I am doing really well, by God's grace," he replied. "How is the family?" Rose inquired.

"They are equally as well," Fred replied.

Children with an abundance of energy darted in and out of the assembly of people. They played any number of games but seemed to enjoy tag the most. They had no care for what, where, or why they were in the massed crowd of people.

"Well, ladies, I would like to continue this morning interlude, but duty requires my absolute attention," he said.

"We just wanted to wish you well. You are all doing a fine job dealing with us," said Rose.

"Always ready to serve," Fred replied.

Aisha continued her story. "I remember when I was a small girl…"

Fred smiled at the ladies as they continued walking. He slowed his gait to allow a greater separation from the group who always were together. *Give them a chance and Aisha will begin another story,* he laughed within.

Many of the people loudly sang gospel songs, rejoicing in old favorites, "Old Rugged Cross," "Blessed Assurance," "Just a Closer Walk with Thee." It was comforting, particularly to the aged. But the children just loved life and enjoyed being with the other kids.

"Fred?" an unfamiliar voice inquired.

Fred turned around slowly, thinking it was the trio of ladies. He referred to them as the Joyful Trio. They would appear everywhere and at any time. Aisha's voice always announced their presence before their recognition.

"Yes, ma'am," he replied, knowing that he did not recall seeing her or recalling her name.

"You don't know me, do you?" she asked.

"Not so sure," he replied. "I see so many people and some names I forget, I am sorry."

"Not to worry. An old woman is easily forgotten," she said.

"If I have implied in a way that you are unimportant to me, again, I am sorry." Fred was ashamed, and the heat in his face rose.

"Please, Pastor, I am not so important to feel slighted," she responded.

"Everyone is important. I am but a humble man, not a pastor, not a teacher, just a man honoring a request from Pastor Longstreet to assist him," he replied.

"You are a man of great integrity," she said.

"In life, I just try to survive, keep my family safe, and obey God's will," he spoke.

"Many feel you are as important to us as Pastor Longstreet," she said.

He looked at her, now paying full attention. "Ma'am, please sity was available, many requests by the elderly were for companionship. Physical and emotional hinderances were nonexistent.

Pastor Longstreet sent runners to alert his designated leaders to intervene on my behalf. The pastor has been appointed by God to lead this flock, not me. Tell those that utter my name that I am one of them and so shall I remain. Give God the glory and don't waste time admiring a man like me. I am a follower, given responsibilities to assist Pastor Longstreet." He paused. "No more or no less."

"Will you help this old lady with one request, please?" she spoke.

"How may I help you?" he inquired.

"Well, some people are complaining. They want to know where we are going and how long it will take us to get there. And others want a better variety of nourishment, more assortments," she carefully spoke. Looking at Fred, she wanted to gauge his concern. He remained calm and walked beside her, unmoved.

"I think that the pastor addressed these concerns with everyone when we began this journey. I will address your concerns with him when we gather later. And that is my promise." He glanced in her direction as she trod along.

Fred continued walking and paid close attention to her, assuring that he moved at her pace. "The pastor wanted me to be the voice of the people, at least bringing their concerns to him," he offered.

Realizing the lady was no longer beside him, he turned to visually look for her. She had gone. He stepped to one side searching faces, but he did not recognize anyone resembling her. Thinking it odd, he resumed walking.

The lovely weather continued, and the gathering that had journeyed together for more than a week appeared to be satisfied that they were headed for a great reward. The children, along with their new friends, were impervious to their surroundings and were devoted entirely to their free time, which appeared always; even the family time mandated by their parents did not deter them from seeking out new adventures. Unknown to them were the elders who assumed constant security and surveillance.

Young men and their families watched the elders and came readily when their services were required. Since almost every necespass the message on to the flock of believers that they should prepare for their midday break. The flock would gather into large groups, mainly groups that had become familiar with the other group members. Grant had asked his assistants to rotate group members to avoid self-imposed isolations. He was cognizant of human emotions, and although he assumed there were no conscious efforts to discriminate for any reason, these were people with personal bias that could create personal isolations. He knew that the devil and his acolytes were on the prowl.

There had been rumblings within the crowd, whose origin was yet unknown. Some were complaining about the sojourn, others about meatless meals, and others about the constant trek into the unknown. Some wondered aloud, Did Pastor Longstreet really know where he was headed?

Rabbi Moshen Levi, Fred Maynard, and Pastor Longstreet watched from raised ground as the people milled around, gathering for their noon supplication before eating. Those who volunteered as servers delivered the meals as they had all the others prior to this time. Baskets filled with fresh rolls, bread, bagels, and other wheats, delectable fruits and vegetables, and cool, body-refreshing water. The sustenance was plentiful.

"I have received an admonishment from within that the great devourer and his minions are infiltrating our flock and are seeking to crack our foundation. Beware of minor discord and constant complaints. These may not be earthly dissidents but minions of Satan," said Pastor Longstreet while rubbing his temple.

Fred Maynard, recalling a strange meeting this morning, spoke. "Pastor, this morning, a lady approached me asking questions that caused me concern. I was polite, but when I sought to speak with her, she appeared to have disappeared."

Rabbi Levi noted to the two, "I observed both Muslims and Jewish members seemingly avoiding each other and settling in isolated groups." A jolt of warm wind swept over him. It was like a strong and assertive force dedicated to toppling him over.

Pastor Longstreet asked, "What do you make of it?"

"I don't really know, it could be an assault on the gathered worshipers by adverse forces," he replied.

"It does appear that evil forces are creating ripples in our group. After everyone has eaten and rested, let us assemble the holy together and address our concerns," suggested Pastor Longstreet. "After eating, walk among the people and let them know that we will remain here awhile."

"It will be as you wish, Pastor Longstreet," said Moshen as he and Fred departed the trio to join their families.

CHAPTER 49

Al Lost had become quite busy of late. He decided that he had to become more hands on with his job, no more allowing others to mold his destiny. *Firsthand guidance is what is required with total loyalty, or face my wrath.*

"I must destroy those that sojourn with Pastor Grant Longstreet. Somehow their destruction will ingratiate me with the master, and I again shall wield my authority with imprudence since there will be no fear of reprisals." He snickered. "Once the master is satisfied, I shall do as I please. I will personally satiate my discomfort in the death of Paul. His success is my failure and eternal death. So where is John Pickney?" he wondered aloud. "His services are required," said Al.

Al Lost found John entertaining a group of restaurant patrons who had joined him at his table. He was joyful today, having received another financial gain in his bank account, which had suddenly grown to an enormous amount. There was no need to be conservative, and the once frugal money manager now spent freely.

"You boys want another round, more food? You know it's on me." He laughed.

A motioning hand to the manager brought another round of both drinks and finger food. There was no reluctance on behalf of the staff, who knew that they would be rewarded significantly. Many had waited on John before and spoke of his generosity when tipping.

"Now where were we?" he asked before he lapsed into another story filled with facts that were enhanced with colorful speech. With the troubles of the world long behind him, money had given a new look at life.

"Hey, tell us about Pastor Longstreet, that charlatan." The question caused loud laughter to erupt. Everyone knew John and Pastor Longstreet, once intimate friends, had parted ways under less-than-desirable circumstances. Someone knew it would give him a charge.

"That godless heathen," responded John, simultaneously sipping his drink. "Yeah, our entire community confided in him for years and he left us alone, high and dry. He did not even have the courtesy to explain why he left us, well at least to our satisfaction."

Al Lost sat behind the group who had occupied all the seats surrounding the table. With little effort he permeated the minds of those that were seated. Many had been enslaved by their delectable alcohol and recreational drugs. Their minds were easily opened to suggestion.

"Pastors, preachers are all deceivers causing contention. They are creating false gods to lament over while your earthly conditions are less than pleasurable. Look how they live at your expense, free of worry or money issues, while many of you lose your entire fortune," whispered Al.

A burly gentleman sneered, "John, I feel your disdain, you give them years of devotion and praise, and when you need them, they pack up and are gone."

Another chimed in, "One of those guys stole my wife from under my nose. I entertained him at my home and my children adored him. That's a fine *how do you do,* they just got up and left."

Al fought hard to resist bursting into laughter. They were like puppets dangling by a masterful puppeteer. *See how they dance.*

John noticed his new friend. "Hey, Al, come closer. Hey, boys, make way for my friend." John waved his hand, motioning away the seated to allow room for Al Lost. Someone passed a chair forward, and others slammed the seat down.

The crowd slapped Al on his back, happy to meet John's friend.

Emboldened by his friend's presence, John bought another round of drinks and asked for some space that he might talk with his friend. The rowdy crowd, inspired by John's stories, happily complied. Many shook hands with the two friends as they made their way to the bar or returned to their original seats prior to gathering around John.

"Good people," stated John.

Al laughed and said, "You have done very well, my friend.

Thank your benefactor for his faith in you."

"I am thankful every single day that he has given me the opportunity to enjoy living," said John. He was living a life that he could not have ever imagined. Valuables upon valuables, friends, and all desires that money guaranteed.

"One would be foolish not to praise the one which made this possible. I am certainly not foolish."

"Glad that you are enjoying your good fortune. It reflects highly on your character," said Lost.

John blushed. A grotesque horror overlayed Al Lost's face; spittle splattered him. He was fighting back deep emotions but held in check by years of training. John, normally boastful when inebriated, was uncharacteristically reticent.

"Friend, and I call you friend because that is what you are, a friend." Allowing the words to sink into the soul of John Pickney, Al Lost slipped and hissed. Did anyone hear that? he thought.

"Well, John, there is a small favor that I need," he asked. "Name it and it is done," replied John.

"Our benefactor has made me aware that your old friend intends on carrying out a drastic deed. Information has come to him that Grant intends on carrying out a plan to kill a massive number of people. He has so enthralled his followers that he is assuring them a better life after their departure." Al paused while assessing the effects of this revelation. "Lives will be lost and families left in lamenting remorse."

"What can I do?" asked John. "We must stop this pending atrocity."

"I adamantly agree," responded Lost.

Ominous fluffy gray clouds that had been gathering outside when Al entered the establishment now roared, seemingly in approval of what was transpiring below. An unrelenting downpour ensued, heightened with crackling, revenging lightning.

Al Lost whispered, "Thank you, my lord, for your approval."

A little wobbly but still coherent, John joined Al departing the establishment, John still sipping on a drink he carried with him. He had given thought to his appearance and demeanor and brushed at his clothes and looked straight ahead.

Al proceeded him to his vehicle and insisted that he drive, which John concurred without argument. "Rest, my friend," Al encouraged John. "We have to journey awhile before catching up with Grant. Be assured we will overtake him, so rest now."

Seating himself in his luxury automobile on the passenger's side, John reclined his seat and leaned back. Sleep immediately subdued him.

Al Lost smiled again, visualizing the rewards that would certainly be bestowed upon him. New and greater authority, command over the dark legions, and alone on top without peers.

CHAPTER 50

Paul met with Mary Louise on the military installation in Texas. He was struggling mentally with the loss of his dear friends, and now he had to convey the story to Mary. He wondered how she was getting along after he departed her company only hours earlier.

The base was large but not overly populated. It was noted for being the medical center for the military and most noted for its burn center. Holding detainees seemed rather odd, but the multifunctional military had personnel to perform multiple tasks.

The military was like a nation within a nation. It functioned perfectly without civilian interference, but recently had lost some of its autonomy as civilians sought to socialize it. Many of the traditions were slowly being changed by many that had never given the ranks a second thought. But expediency allowed them to join the ranks of the changers.

They will eventually carve away the core values, and it will be run by vagabonds, thought Paul.

He was very proud of the time he had given the nation. It had grounded him, given him a job, and prepared him for life. How that had been altered by his current endeavors never reflected on how he loved the military.

Angel Concepcion awoke from a semiconscious mental state while lying on a much-used mattress. He was jolted awake by some unknown stimulus. Looking around for someone, he saw nothing. He felt like he was caged in this eight-by-eight cell, few visitors, and they were all stockade guards. Angel longed to see his family. He could manage the imprisonment, but not seeing his spouse and daughter really played games with his mind.

Wondering why he had come to the United States troubled him. He was satisfied with his humble life in Mexico. He worked, and his spouse tended the house and raised his daughter. Friends stopped by nearly daily, and he longed for the Sunday gatherings to preach the Gospel to members of his small community. They enjoyed friendship and personal interactions at each gathering.

A voice had come to him while he toiled at his construction job. It was a voice that had startled him. *Your presence is required in Kansas, near Topeka. Gather your family and meet with Pastor Longstreet. He is traveling with a gathering of believers.*

The power of the suggestion had appeared so vivid as if the person talking was near him, although his visual scanning of the immediate area disclosed no one.

So along with his family, he headed north into the United States inspired by only a mental urging. His spouse, who prayed daily and often never doubted him, followed his direction. Angel had entered the United States multiple times without incident and had no reservation about traveling across the border.

He and his family met his cousin in Corpus Christi, Texas, and was driven to San Antonio in his cousin's van. However, US Customs agents had been alerted to vans transporting noncitizens into the United States. While stopping for gas and refreshments, they were arrested.

Fort Sam Houston, a military installation in San Antonio, Texas, had facilities for illegal aliens where they were processed and detained until they would be returned back across the border. They separated the children and women and processed them separately. Often families that were separated were never regrouped together and their return to their parent countries were disjointed and problematic.

Angel Concepcion was in the process of returning to Mexico, hoping to join his family there. His inquiries into their whereabouts had fallen on deaf ears. So here he waited in silence. *Why has God led me here to be returned to Mexico, and where is my family?* he thought.

Mary Louise was tired, hungry, and mentally exhausted. Her clothes were damp with the day's sweat, which ran down natural crevices on her body. She was miserable. When she saw Paul, tears welled in her eyes. All the tribulations of the day had gathered en masse and unrelentingly assaulted her mind. She was totally exhausted.

Paul moved to her side and smiled his unassuming smile, natural and sincere. Without inquiring, he suggested that they get something to eat. How would he tell her about Rebecca and Daniel? That could wait. She appeared to need some time to rest.

An eatery with multiple stores separated by partitions housed the various venders. Many people, young, old, military trainees, retired personnel, and families dined on nationally established food chains. It was wide and loud enough to shield everyone's conversation, and left the patrons, who were plentiful, freedom to commune.

Mary Louise just wanted to eat and find a place to sleep. She was totally drained by the day's fiasco. She felt that nothing had been accomplished. She wanted to go home.

"What do you want to eat, Mary Louise?" Paul asked.

"Pizza and a soda," she said, rubbing her neck. "And I don't care what flavor. Please add a bottle of water."

"Got it." Paul turned and walked toward the pizza shop.

They enjoyed the small meal, which invigorated Mary Louise. She felt much better, and the gripping pains in her belly subsided. She looked at Paul, who appeared to be in deep thought. "What are you thinking about, friend?" she asked.

"Well, I have something that I need to tell you." He appeared subdued. He paused, seemingly seeking the proper words.

"Spit it out," she said halfway jokingly. She turned toward him, fully engaging him with her eyes.

"Rebecca and Daniel are dead," he responded. There was no hesitation, no conscious thought, just the terse statement.

"Don't joke like that!" she shouted.

"I wish it were a joke, I wish I were at some other place at some other time in my life. I wish a lot," he replied. Returning her gaze, he said, "But I am left here with you and to some fate I have no control over."

"How did they die, Paul?" she asked, fighting back the tears in her burning eyes.

"I am not exactly sure; however, I suspect it was something mutual. They died sitting together on the couch. There appeared to be something out of the ordinary—evil, I suspect." Tears surfaced in his eyes.

"These are some ungodly times," she replied. Mary wanted to embrace Paul but decided not to.

Paul walked in silence as they headed to where Angel Concepcion was being detained. They walked for several blocks, passing several military personnel attired in their requisite service uniforms. Some walked in file while others moved purposely in all directions.

Mary Louise recollected times at home helping her mother tend the garden and her flower arrangements while working diligently under the large magnolia trees that shaded their property. The walks through her neighborhood with her father greeting neighbors they met along the way caused her to smile. She saw the black and brown workers moving about engaged in laughter, solid people, but reticent when the homeowners were around. Their warmth between each other was inspiring, but she could not figure out why it changed when the homeowners were around.

She recalled how the black and brown people avoided each other and pretended they were hard at work when police officials were around. She had known these police officers since she was a small child, and they always seemed overly nice when speaking with her parents or casting a glance her way. *v*

"This is the place, Paul, they are contained here," said Mary Louise.

CHAPTER 51

The crowd of followers momentarily mingled together, surrounding Pastor Longstreet. Some searched for their children, who had wandered into the crowd seeking friends they spent much of their time with, enjoying whatever activities that they could.

"I am cognizant of the frequent grumblings among you, the separation into groups while purposely avoiding others. The disdain for your sustenance that is always ready to be consumed when it is time. I hear your complaints, it saddens me, it sickens me deep into my very soul that in such a short time we are trying to regress."

He continued, "You have come to me freely to journey together as brothers and sisters in Christ and to make this journey into the unknown of your own free will. You gave up everything, everything was left behind. All your baggage, earthly possessions, and memories, all left behind. It was by faith that you joined together to venture into the unknown. God called and you came." Pastor Longstreet was constantly turning about as he spoke to face everyone who had gathered. "I do not know where we are going or when we will reach there,

but it is by my faith and my faith alone that I now travel this path as your guide." Tears filled his eyes, hurt by his lack of more substantial information, while watching the gathered people sheepishly wonder why Pastor Longstreet had assembled them today.

They knew that what he was saying was as he had explained to them in the beginning—nothing had changed.

"Amongst you are some that want this movement to fail. They are the unholy lions that seek to consume you. They rely on inuendo, lies, and deceit to splinter you. They seek the weak, the doubtful, those that know the truth but question their own inner feelings. There are no different races here, no different ethnicities, no poor or rich." He turned about. "No Christians, no Jews, no Muslims, no Hindus, there are only God's children traveling together. We have faced animals, perilous weather, and frightful beings that falsely attack you and yet who has been harmed? I would like to eat steaks and have ice cream for dessert, but I get by with what is being provided."

The same old lady that had approached Fred earlier resurfaced at the front of the crowd. Her smirk filled with hatred colored her face. "Pastor," she said. The crowd looked in her direction, everyone recognized her voice, but no one recognized her appearance. What was her name? they asked one another. They knew her, they thought, but did they?

"Pastor," she repeated.

Pastor Longstreet looked in her direction, and he alone could see the demon within. *To what purpose is she here?* he thought.

"Pastor, I am but an elderly lady following along with help and the hope to finish this journey. I know you are a man sent to us by someone, but who, I do not know."

What is she going to say now? She's preparing a statement which will confuse the crowd. He glared at her, knowing that she was an agent of the Great Deceiver. God had given him discernment, and he knew to be aware of this thing.

"Did you not belong to a racial hatred group that killed black people and persecuted Jewish families? How is it now that you speak of the equality of people when you do not really believe that yourself, Pastor Longstreet?"

"What I did as a youth, I cannot undo. I cannot heal a wrong with a mere explanation. I have been forgiven by the person I harmed and by the Living God. Everyone here knows that. I am going to call you out right here and now, agent of Satan, get behind me, Satan. I rebuke you in Jesus's name!"

As if time had been suspended, the elderly woman sneered and drifted into the crowd, assuming a different guise. She had not been defeated, just slowed. She looked toward the pastor and giggled. "I am not done."

Pastor Longstreet continued, "Now, fellow believers, let us gather together and venture forward. Stay vigilant, my friends, the enemy is alive and willing to corrupt you, take your minds off the prize. Even when I confront one wrong, many more materialize and all are bordering on chaos. Let us pray."

Continuing further, Pastor Longstreet said, "Followers of God love their brothers and sisters regardless of their earthly situations, they don't hate because of their skin's melanin," looking around at the flock of believers. "They don't hate because of their economic status. They don't hate because their brothers have committed crimes which they have repented. They don't hate because of their sexual orientation. God will one day open your eyes and you will no longer be lost. One day you will be called by God and you shall be judged, some will wonder why they are being cast into infamy. They'll plead their case. God may judge them wanting not because they worshipped him, but they inwardly hated their brothers and sisters and judged them unfairly. This journey we undertake you were asked to take by faith alone, I ask you to continue further by faith. Please, I implore you, continue by faith and leave your biases, prejudices, and silliness behind. You will be judged one day, be not wanting. Call on the Living God for strength when troubled. The wandering lion is pleased when you venture from God."

Pastor Longstreet stepped from his grassy perch and left the gathered to rest.

CHAPTER 52

There was no doubt in Paul's mind what he would do. Entering the confinement facility would be easy. Finding the separated family, left to his own faculties, would be a bit more challenging. But this was not his tasking.

"Mary, you must find Angel Concepcion while I seek out his family. I do not know if they are together or if the children have separated," said Paul. "Meet me outside of the fence line." Paul pointed toward an area not fully lit, slightly shaded by a nonfunctioning light that had not been repaired. Paul entered his transport cloud.

Entering the facility's administrative office with several military personnel performing a variety of functions, walking about, she was confronted by a sergeant, who sat behind a huge oak desk. "How may I help you?" he asked.

She would not engage in deceit and spoke, "I have come for Angel Concepcion and his family."

"Who is he, ma'am?" he asked.

"He is being detained here by you, and I need for you to release him to me."

"By what authority?" he asked, now standing. He was a slim, physically built man, but emboldened by his authority, he stood firm.

Confident but not totally assured what would transpire, feeling a degree of mental fear, Mary repositioned her feet, seeking more stability. "By the authority of the Living God," she said boldly.

The military personnel who had been moving about all stopped and looked toward the brewing confrontation. They were confident in their sergeant but curious to see what he would do. "PFC Henderson, call the military police and alert CID," spoke the sergeant. "Morales and Mayer, detain her," he ordered.

Mary Louise now faced an immediate confrontation that she had not figured on. She sought to place her hand into her pockets to assure them that she was not a threat to them. It was too late. She felt her body being slammed against the wall. She lost air. A darkness fought against consciousness. She did not want to faint.

Two soldiers physically restrained her. Their grips bit into her arms, creating an immediate, overwhelming confusion that overcame her. She wanted to run to get away but could not free herself.

Mary Louise stood up somehow. She had freed herself from the vice grips of the two military soldiers. They stared in her direction, and all of the other personnel in the room were looking in her direction but were not moving. Concern was on their faces, and their concern was her.

Mary Louise stood without the physical restraints. There was nothing inhibiting her motion; however, everything around her had stopped. Suspended in some unknown restraint, she moved forward, scanning the room left and right, but nothing impeded her. *He is in the back,* an unknown whisper pierced her mind. This was supernatural, but these were strange days.

She entered the cell block area, whereas in the outside room everything remained motionless. How would she find him? she asked herself. And how much time did she have? *I'll call his name,* she thought, *it can't hurt.* "Angel Concepcion? Mr. Concepcion?"

An unknown voice responded, "I am here."

Mary hurriedly made her way through the maze of corridors containing the cell blocks, constantly scanning her surroundings. In the distance, a man was moving, his hands grasping the steel bars. "I am Angel," he said.

As Mary Louise approached the cell, the door opened. "Come quickly, please," she spoke.

"Who are you?" he inquired.

"I just don't have the time to explain this to you, but you must hurry, just follow me," she said.

"I will not leave here without my wife and child," he replied. "They are being removed from this block as we speak," she

stated.

"I want to see them now," he replied.

"Look around you, sir. This is not normal, and you must agree, whatever is happening is for your benefit, and for how long, I don't know. Now please hurry."

Reluctantly, he followed her, all along wondering why everything and everybody was motionless. What power held everyone at bay? He knew something diabolical was about. A maleficent presence hovered in the dark. He fought against the nauseous feeling that emerged.

"Come. Quickly." Mary Louise beckoned as she led him from the cell block. Everything remained in suspension as she headed out of the facility. Mary Louise remembered the prearranged meeting place, and with Mary Louise leading, they headed directly there.

Angel sped up, noticing his family accompanied by a stranger standing only several feet away. Angel rambled forward, nearly tripping over feet, rapidly moving feet. Angel and his family had a hardy embrace. "That was really wild," said Mary Louise. "You won't believe what just happened," she said.

"I can only imagine," responded Paul. "I bet you can." She smiled.

"We must hurry," said Paul. "Mary Louise, you must get a car and take them to Topeka, Kansas. It is important that you travel quickly, I think something important is amiss. People, let's go, the soldiers will be coming soon and all sort of alerts will follow."

They moved rapidly away from the facilities and headed away. Paul had no idea where he was going. Wondering why he could not carry the gathered in his cloud transportation, he stumbled along with the group. They suddenly slowed.

A male figure casually approached them. He was not anxious nor appeared to have any concern other than to greet them. "Is there a Paul and Mary Louise here?" he asked.

Paul, assuming responsibility for the group, answered, "My name is Paul."

"I am Walker Grabowski, and I have these car keys for you. The reason I am here is that I fell asleep earlier this evening while watching television and I dreamed a dream so real I believed I was awake. A great bright angelic being appeared before me and directed me to meet with five believers at this very spot. You can say I was taken aback and figured this was a dream. He told me that I had been chosen by God to assist him. The angel said I needed to give you these keys to my car and that you should leave the keys in the car in a field outside of Topeka, Kansas. You will recognize the field. The field shall have three large crosses, all gold in color with the inscription 'He Has Risen' on them. I did not believe the dream and fell asleep again, and the exact dream represented itself exactly, still I was skeptical and fell asleep again, but the next time I dreamed the same dream, I became a true believer. Please be safe." And without further conversation, Grabowski turned and walked into the night's darkness.

Paul handed the keys to Mary Louise. "You must go now, the authorities will be looking for you and the others, and they may possibly be guided by unnatural forces. Their pursuit may be tenacious and no telling what they will do if you are caught. You are a fugitive now, and a federal fugitive at that. Be safe, be careful. I have a very strange feeling deep inside me that things may be culminating into something awfully bad."

Angel Concepcion and his family were trying to grasp what they were seeing and kneeled to offer prayer. Whatever they had been drawn into appeared to be directed by the All Mighty, and they would bow in respect and supplication.

They watched as a cloud descended and Paul stepped into it and vanished. "What a great God! How honored are we."

Mary Louise hugged Angel, his wife, and his daughter. "We must be going." Alarms rang out loudly.

CHAPTER 53

Al Lost and John Pickney drove along the interstate heading toward Missouri. The journey went on uneventful other than the frequent and constant lambasting of Pastor Longstreet.

Al spoke, "I hope we are not too late for the benefit of those lost souls who are following that monster. Will he sacrifice the lives of those who have given up their entire belongings to follow him into whatever hell or false god that he worships?"

"We must proceed now with all haste to interrupt him. There are women, children, and others who are lost," replied John. "We are morally responsible to stop this."

"Yes, my friend, now that you have returned to the living, you see our mission clearly," replied Al. "Our mission is righteous. We on this day will please our master and he shall reward us with riches beyond belief. I can guarantee that, my friend."

"I am certainly ready to meet the benefactor who has been so gracious to me. He has loved me without meeting with me personally," said John.

"I tell you, this very day the master shall be in his home and he shall receive you with open arms. There you shall see the multitude who followed his desires and are in his presence weeping and praising him. You shall be one with them," spoke Al. "This I can assure you." John leaned back and received the statements from his friend.

How he had been blessed. He recalled as a youth that he was tormented by his father, who repeatedly told him that he would be nothing more than a bum. How he had fooled him. He was financially sound and would receive even greater rewards. How good is life? he thought.

CHAPTER 54

Into the travel cloud and soon in his apartment, not together with friends any longer, no arguments with Rebecca, or long joyful gatherings with Daniel. It was just him now, alone and lost.

Something was amiss. Paul thought, *Why have I not emerged from the cloud? Am I in limbo?* Paul could not tell if he had even moved. The still was just that, a stillness, no noise, just a soundless, motionless vacuum. He pondered, *Has my time ended? Have I completed everything I had to do? Where to now?*

He told himself to relax, to be patient, and one way or the other something would happen.

There was nothing left to do but to accept things as they were, and for what it was, being alone lost in time. *Just relax,* he willed, but that was not so easily achieved. In this reality, that was all he had to do, his only quest. *Just relax,* he repeated.

Mary Louise drove up the interstate highway heading north. She traveled through Oklahoma and crossed into Kansas. There had not been any incidents, no police, no pursuits, and everything was proceeding without incident. There was a series of uncommon events that had her concerned. The car's electrical system failed, and fortunately a road mechanic had assisted them to remedy the issue, a failed alternator. Two tires had leaks in them and were replaced; however, they were not balanced, and the vehicle bucked when exceeding fifty miles per hour.

They had stopped to eat, and the car battery failed. *What next?* she wondered, but nothing went wrong.

Angel was very inquisitive, asking more questions than she had answers for, but otherwise, the trip went well. Angel's daughter, Elise, spoke English well enough to keep her entertained, and when Mary Louise slept, the young lady joined her in the back of the car and slept as well.

Angel relieved Mary Louise and shared time behind the wheel. Mary Louise thought to herself, everything was proceeding without incident and soon all the answers would be known.

Elise reminded her of Charlotte, so innocent and charming. In another life, they would have been great childhood friends, she thought.

A large field located along Interstate 335 was divided by a continuous row of trees. The field appeared to be symmetrically divided, rows of amber grain that swayed with the wind created a picturesque image. Three gold crosses stood tall and magnificent. Mary Louise thought, *What a glorious sight!*

"Hey, wake up, everyone. I think we are here," she said as she slowed the vehicle and traveled off road on a dusty, unpaved country road. "Gather what you have, and we will just wait here," she instructed her companions. "Pastor Longstreet should be here soon." The small group sought out shade along the tree line. They huddled together awaiting the pastor. A flock of birds landed in the fields forging for the many insects that were likewise eating away at the plentiful vegetation. It was like a never-ending cycle, life to death and death to life.

CHAPTER 55

One thing that never daunted the children was the long, tedious journey. Each mile, each day was another adventure for the children. There was no housework, no homework, and no parents riding herd over them. They were basically free to roam, and that was what they did very well.

Games on games, some created, some known, but all entertaining. Where they had come from or where they were going was all the same, and they loved the adventure.

To the parents, it was another day like many before, walking, eating, and talking and making acquaintances. The accommodations had proven sufficient for the wanderers. They longed for or actually needed little. Young and old on blind faith trekked across several states following their leader, unnerved.

Sister Rose, Valerie, and Aisha had taken it upon themselves to care for the children during the daylight hours while their parents were occupied with other tasks. All the adults cared for each other and offered assistance when needed.

Sister Rose and Valerie were always in great spirits listening to some outlandish stories offered by their friend, Aisha. She told so many stories in a day but never repeated any, although she intermingled facts between them. They were all entertaining, and the listeners waited in anticipation for the next one.

In the evenings, the children gathered around to listen to her renditions of timely fairy tales, which she told with clarity and filled with ample visible illusions that kept them captivated. After each story, the children clamored for more and were disappointed when their parents retrieved them. But promises of new stories softened their disappointments.

As for Pastor Longstreet, he felt their long journey was finally ending, nothing specific, but an inner feeling that the trip's conclusion was nearing. He had listened to the complaints and had been an arbitrator for concerns between families and religious leaders for the thousands. The weight of the days had not deterred him, for he was confident that God would provide.

The guiding light was leading him toward a long row of trees that divided the large field of golden grain. So magnificent was the tree line among the grain that its beauty was indescribable. The grain swayed in the wind; it was a bit mesmerizing. Pastor Longstreet decided that this would be a great place to rest.

As the group went through their never-ending ritual of gathering for meals, volunteers gathered the refreshments, and blankets were laid out beneath the shading tree canopies. It was more difficult to gather the children together and link them with their families. There was concern that families could not find their children, but many had not been overly concerned.

Many had consumed their meals and set aside food for the missing children. Food was never to be stored and all the food had to be eaten as directed by Pastor Longstreet. Some had attempted to defy the order, and the food immediately rotted and became infested with maggots.

Unknown to Pastor Longstreet, he was only less than a quarter of a mile from the three golden crosses where the assembled group would assume their journey. He was wondering if they should continue or just stay here for the remainder of the day.

Fred Maynard approached him and said, "Pastor, some of the children cannot be located and missed the noon meal." He appeared excited because his children were also missing.

"How are your kids?" Pastor Longstreet asked.

"We cannot find them. They are also missing," replied Fred.

"Have you spoken with Sister Rose? She normally always has knowledge of the whereabouts of the children," said Pastor Longstreet. "I have spoken with her and she has not seen them. Something

odd, Aisha, her constant companion, is also unaccounted for," said Fred.

"Contact Rabbi Levi and let us have an assembly and have everyone account for others that are traveling with them. Gather a list of the unaccounted and we will proceed from there. Keep everyone together."

The concern in Pastor Longstreet's voice was apparent. He thought this particular place appeared out of the ordinary. *What surprises are awaiting us here?* he thought.

CHAPTER 56

Angel Concepcion walked into the woods. He had grown restless just sitting there. He was not unhappy to be there, just restless. He walked, looking at the trees arrayed together in perfect harmony. No worries or concerns, just together in one accord. *Isn't God great?* he thought.

Leaves and pine needles covered the ground, and along with the arrangement of the trees, created a natural pathway. It had not been frequently traveled or ever traveled because nothing appeared disturbed. Angel continued walking, but soon became nauseated. He stepped backward and felt better. Something in these trees beyond where he was, was unholy.

Angel looked to his left, then to his right, and the tree line extended further than he believed. The sun's light had difficulty piercing the trees. He forced himself forward, fighting against strong discouraging doubt. The trees appeared alive and resisted his advances, but he was not deterred. He fought against the puncturing needles and harsh tree bark. It even seemed as if the trees moved, restricting his movement. He remained adamant. Something was encouraging him to continue.

Angel struggled against the unholy, restricting vegetation, encouraged by an unseen voice that urged him forward. An odious, repugnant smell pierced him like a thrusting rapier. He was near exhaustion, feeling as if he were carrying another fifty pounds of weight on his body, but there was none. Struggling against the mental onslaught, his resolve grew even greater. *Whatever wants me to fail must not want me to succeed.* He wondered, *What is ahead that I should not see?*

Somehow, Angel made his way, and as he came closer, he saw exactly what he expected, some duplicitous creature indwelling within a host. There were others. Many children were entranced, looking into some abyss enticing themselves with desires they had not ever known. They appeared as puppets being dangled. There was no fright, only apparent acquiescence.

A lady stood in their midst. Her soul was struggling, but the demonic host held on tenaciously. Alone, she had not the power to overcome this, her possession. Angel broke free of the vegetative barrier and called to the evil, "In God's name, free the lady!"

"I don't want to do that, priest! She is mine, along with her little friends. The master will be well pleased. Be gone, or you shall become a victim of being in the wrong place at the wrong time!"

"In the powerful name of Jesus," he said, "get behind me, Satan!" The priest was fearless as he slowly approached the abomination. "Release her! God commands you!"

"You are not God, just a lowly priest who God does not even know. Why are you risking destruction for them? She is only a lonesome soul! Nothing more. Not worth anything to anyone."

"In the name of God, be gone, demon! Release her!" said Angel, more emphatically now. "In Jesus's name, release her, you diabolical spawn!"

"I will kill the kids now, if you do not leave me alone!" The entity made some hand gesture, and the children appeared to be burning. "Now see what you caused me to do, priest!"

"In the name of Jesus, release them, devil!" continued the priest.

He would not entertain the demon with useless conversation.

An angel appeared behind Angel Concepcion with a flaming sword. Fearlessly, he stood tall and intimidating. The demon shuddered.

"Priest, you disappoint me! You are no match for me, so you solicit the favor of the Highest and conjure up his warriors. One hundred angels appear with you against me, a single adversary."

Angel had no idea what the demon spoke of, and it had to be some trick, another diabolical attempt to seduce him. Angel stayed the course.

"In the name of the Living God, release her!" he commanded. His faith grew even stronger. *For this moment I was born!*

"We shall meet again, priest, but the next time I shall have the advantage of a number of my minions, and you shall not escape. I will personally torment you for eternity!" the demon sneered.

"Be gone, demon! In Jesus's name, depart!"

"There shall be a time of my revenge," sneered the demon. There was no need to continue this conversation, thought

Angel. *He needs me to validate him.* He moved toward the lady to offer assistance.

"Sir, who are you, and where did you come from?" asked Aisha. "I am a lowly priest, Angel Concepcion, who along with my family and a friend are sitting over there awaiting a friend."

The children ran from the woods as jovial as always, seeking new adventures.

"Well, I am Aisha, journeying with Pastor Longstreet and an assembly of God's followers. Where we are going, I can't say, but we are certainly nearer, and I am sure you would be welcomed to join us. At least have lunch," she said.

Aisha had not known it, but others were looking for her and the children. They had already eaten.

Angel told Aisha that he would meet with his companions, and if they were willing, they would join them directly. She returned to the group and submitted to numerous questions. She was taken aback and wondered out loud what was the basis for their concern since they had never really left the group. She stated she was gathering the children from the woods and never lost sight of the group.

Mary Louise and her friends emerged from the woods. She immediately recognized Pastor Longstreet and introduced herself, Angel Concepcion, and his family. She had seen Longstreet several times on television.

After explaining how she had come to be here at this specific time, Grant explained to her how he was directed to meet them here near the golden painted crosses.

CHAPTER 57

Paul emerged from the cloud and watched the proceedings. He saw the gathered people jubilantly move toward their journey's end. Elation filled him. Reveling in what appeared to be the culmination of his journey felt rewarding. Maybe Lena would be on the other side of the state line, and he would once again feel the warmth that she provided. How he longed to see her again.

Pastor Longstreet stood alongside the following that had traveled with him across the country. He searched for some familiar faces that he hoped would be with the gathering, people he had encountered while traveling his life's path. Hearing his internal voice, he was now made fully aware of his purpose in escorting these followers on this journey.

The faithful walked onward, singing loud a hymn of praise. So joyful was their victorious voices that their sound echoed in the far distance. The long journey would end today. The rewards that had been promised had created new personal friendships. When they were not laughing, they were engaged in jesting with their friends that they had created profound personal bonds. No sadness, no worries, young and old traveled, some holding hands; totally content, they walked.

Pastor Longstreet climbed a small hill, fingering five smooth stones that he had picked during the journey. They held no mysteries, but appeared to calm his mind when it was troubled. He had at times carried stones in his pockets for mental calmness, but considered that they would offend God. Belief in God should suffice.

The sun had risen high in the sky and cast its ever-present view for some distance. Its warmth filled the excited group to an even greater excitement. Everyone and everything appeared to be in perfect harmony.

"You have done a wonderful job, Pastor Longstreet," a soft feminine voice broke his silence.

"Mary Louise," he answered, not startled, but the suddenness of her had interrupted his peace. "It surely was the work of God. Give him the praise."

"I do every day," she replied. She gripped her hands lightly and drew them to her lips. These last several weeks had been challenging, but the final solution appeared within range.

"So, my child, what brings you here? You should be rejoicing with the young people, the saved."

She was overwhelmed, and excitement encompassed her very soul. "I would, Pastor, but soon something wonderful could occur and I may just burst into sheer joy. It might just burst me into uncontrollable joy, and my feelings might just burst free like an uncontrollable flame."

They grasped hands and hugged a friendly gesture of joy. Grant, while in Mary Louise's grasp, noticed a strange black-

ness in the distance. The sky was bright, void of obvious clouds, but strange darkness hovered below, blotting out the sun's radiance. Peace truly appeared to have eluded the group because what was rapidly gaining on them did not appear to be beneficent.

John Pickney and Al Lost sped along the near-straight cement highway, easily exceeding the posted speed limits. Tall amber grass strands waved, enhanced by the speeding metal vehicle. John was fully aware of his mission, and he was fully capable of completing it.

Al remained silent, but whispered in the mind of John, who was so infuriated with Grant Longstreet that it did not take much to incite him. He felt deeply offended by the pastor, totally hurt, betrayed. His retribution would be fast and furious.

He had longed for revenge over several months; now it appeared to come to fruition.

Al, overwhelmed with unholy elation, could barely retain his human disguise, struggling mightily against his demonic indwelling. Sulfuric spittle splattered from his snarling lips. A hissing sound remained bound, but only slightly.

"I think Grant is over there." John pointed. "Yeah, that is him," he continued, "and I am headed there." He rambled across the road at full speed, yelling and screaming, "Deceiver, blasphemer, liar!" He was now uncontained.

Al Lost could no longer retain his true form and burst forward. He vacated the speeding auto and rose high in the sky, shouting hatred and blasphemies. He spoke words of magic that allowed a dark horde to manifest in the earthly dimension. The swarm materialized.

The faithful lacked courage and scrambled in the direction they were heading. They left what little belongings they carried, and headed as far away as they could from the dark horde on the road. They held tightly to their families. Pulling, pushing, and screaming, beckoning everyone forward, they ran.

The great demon, Satan's taskmaster, directed the minions of hell toward their foe. Excitement overcame the taskmaster, for in his mind he would be exalted by his master, Satan. God's plan would be altered, and the fallacy of his prophecies would be made plain.

Look at those tiny, puny people scramble, but their demise is assured. Maybe I'll bargain for their souls, a kind of arbitrator, and they, out of their appreciation, will secretly worship me. My status will increase even more within our realm. His mind was rambling with visions of grandeur.

The great demon found renewed humor while watching God's faithful scream and shout for help. There would be no help because their fate was sealed.

The horde of minions gathered behind the great taskmaster, readying to pounce on their foe. As a collective, the minions were an imposing foe, with their increasing capricious hunger enhancing. A frothy secretion of sulfuric saliva welled in the horde. They would soon gather souls for their master.

John's peripheral vision left him, and his companion's departure had nearly gone unnoticed. He blindly drove his vehicle forward, erasing the distance that separated him from his prey. *Soon*, he thought, *very soon that charlatan would be in my clutches.*

Mary Louise, with excitement spiraling, turned to face the iron vehicle, which rambled unabated toward them, and very soon neared them. She noticed Paul scrambling up the hill, grasping for air to fill his burning lungs. He had noticed the vehicle screaming in the distance toward Pastor Longstreet minutes before.

Mary Louise ran toward the vehicle and yelled to Pastor Longstreet, "Move!" As her last words rang out on the mortal plane, the rambling vehicle slammed into her small body. The impact killed her instantly.

The vehicle rested immediately after the impact. John vaulted from the vehicle with his 40 mm handgun raised to shoulder. He did not hesitate and fired several rounds toward Pastor Longstreet.

Paul, who was witnessing the events on the hill, rushed as rapidly as he could to intercede. He vaulted himself into the air to shield the pastor. Paul received a mortal wound to his head while pushing Grant down the opposite side of the hill. Within moments, he thought a seemingly joyful occasion had been overcome by an unholy chaos. He wondered why he was thinking about the events, for surely, he was dead.

As if a blindfold had been removed from the eyes of John, the great demon taskmaster severed his head with a great scimitar. John Pickney's body transformed into one of the demon harbingers that was preparing to assault God's chosen. "What have I done?" he ashamedly asked himself.

"You have done my will, for which I am well pleased," noted the great demon. "I shall reward you. Now we must destroy these interlopers and return home. Onward!" he commanded. Thousands of demons lurked forward, shouting obscenities and blaspheming God. Their fate was sealed, and the wait for God's judgement unbeknownst to them was imminent.

A legion of angels materialized in the sky above the turmoil. They were well armed and appeared well equipped to engage the unhuman rabble they confronted. A command voice quickly rattled out well-thought-out commands while rapidly assessing the battlefield.

The minions slowed almost to a halt. Once spurred by numbers and hatred, they were now confronted by an adversary that appeared unafraid and ready for business.

The mass of followers gathered their composure and scurried onward. They moved rapidly, but less fearful. As the followers cleared into Iowa, appearing to be where their sanctuary was, a transparent barrier arose behind them. Immediately, they were raptured into another dimension housing many mansions, heaven.

Grant had tumbled down the opposite side of the hill, but gathered himself and reclaimed the stability of his feet. He heard and saw the calamity that was occurring around him. He asked himself, *Where is Paul? Where is Mary Louise?*

Scanning around him, he too saw the barrier and noticed many moving headlong toward it. He recognized Fred Maynard standing by the Iowa border, directing the mass of followers onward. Behind him were tumultuous battles enhanced with blasphemies and curses. God's forces had appeared to have gained control and were driving the unholy back into their fiery abyss. John wondered what he was doing and what form he had morphed into, certainly not of a human. A flamed steel blade tore into John, and he screamed. What appeared to be moments and a sensation of falling materialized into an abundance of flaming lakes of fire. John witnessed countless soulless faces reaching for assistance from the torment, and numerous mouths crying for redemption, yet they had no relief and no opportunity of finding any.

John felt he was being pushed with others into this lake of fire. He called out to Al Lost.

The light angel felled the great taskmaster with a withering assault. The taskmaster had no skills to match the skillful swordsmanship of his adversary. The great taskmaster, the evil demon, cried for help. His cries echoed without relief as he returned into his hellish abode.

"Master." He knelt with his head bowed. "I have failed you."

Satan, emotionless, responded, "Join the torment."

The lake of fire opened and received the once great demon, whose body withered and regained his weak human frame. He cried, feeling the fire burn without destroying him. The once number one assistant, with such boastfulness, had now been lowered to just one of many of the countless souls.

CHAPTER 5 8

There was a brilliant light that glowed from the amber field of wheat that clothed the entire plains. Its luminosity was incomparable and stood like a great beacon lighting the way for those soon to be raptured.

Pastor Longstreet had fulfilled his task and now watched the glory of God as the multitude of saints slowly passed before him and fade into glory. The journey had been arduous with numerous struggles, but now they were like past dreams, fading away. They were now behind him.

People followed people, slowly crossing the Iowa state border. What they had left behind, they would regain tenfold. They came from all races that inhabited the earth. There were children, the incredibly old, infirm, healthy, and all had one great desire, and that was to be in the presence of God. Unabated, they made that faithful last step.

The sun stood bright, its glory radiated in all directions, and what had been for Grant Longstreet a period of emotional struggle, had now appeared to have ended. He watched as the faithful vanished before him. Fred and Jiri Maynard, with their children, walked closely by him, their faces wearing an earnest smile, a smile filled with only true love. They had reached the culmination of their journey.

Moshen Levi followed closely behind his colleague. He too smiled frequently, closing his eyes, searching his mind for the promised favor granted to his people by God. A glorious rainbow arched above. *The day of the Lord,* he thought.

There was no longer a guiding light to move him forward, no mass of believers to lead forward, no more doubts. He was worn by the tedious journey and the final assault upon his gathering, and how God had saved them. He cried out, "Your will be done!" The glory of his emotion overwhelmed him. Grant had reached an inner nirvana, unmitigated and all consuming. "How glorious, my God, my God!" He wondered what had happened to Mary Louise. He had only known her briefly before she fell before him. She had sacrificed her life for his, and he was saddened because he might not ever know her fate. In the brief time he had known her, he believed she had a wonderful soul.

He noticed Paul's body laid low on the ground. *I should have some of the faithful help me carry him into the Promised Land. His body should not be left behind.* He cried, recalling how Paul had sacrificed his body for him. *So many people offered themselves to save me, what selflessness.*

As Pastor Longstreet began to walk the short distance where his friend lay low, an angel approached him. "Do not weep for Paul. He is not dead, just mentally injured. God has need of him once more. He will soon arise. Now, Pastor Longstreet, a friend awaits you." Looking in the direction of the border, the angel directed him toward the barrier. He did not speak, but followed the direction of the angel.

Astonished, he saw Mary Louise's petite body standing on the other side of the barrier. She was a glorious light.

Passing over to the other dimension, Grant reached to receive her hand. He grasped the heart and soul of the young lady. "Mary Louise," he said. He tenderly reached toward her, grasping her hand. "We are at the end of our journey, and let us together rise to paradise." She held his outstretched hand tenderly. "I am certainly ready,"

she responded, and together they ascended with a multitude of friends and family. Their journey was complete.

"Rise, Paul, you have things to do. Open your eyes and witness the glory of God," said the angelic host. The angel revealed himself and assumed a human form, his wings hanging downward. "Stand, Paul, you are not dead. Your work is not complete."

Paul rose slowly, still unsteady from the tremendous explosion that pierced him. There was no throbbing pain, but the projectile packed a devastating wallop that was altering his equilibrium. Paul somehow knew he wasn't dead, as he just minutes earlier had observed the same surroundings. He watched the people reach a point and disappear. Paul questioned himself, *Is this the promised destination? Will I be allowed to complete my mysterious sojourn?*

"They tried to alter God's plan, but failed. They will try again and again, because it is their way. I shall clear your vision so that you can also see their futile efforts to curtail this holy plan," spoke the angel.

There were hundreds of thousands of implike beings attempting to assault the mental consciousness of the followers still en route to Iowa. They were cursing, casting illusions, lying, but nothing prevailed. The hideous creatures were powerless against the select people. Greater creatures came, even more grotesque, but they also achieved the same results.

Unknown to the remaining earthly inhabitants, they would soon be deep into the Time of Sorrow. They would be shielding themselves from creatures and events alike while struggling to survive. "Come walk with me, Paul, and I will show you the wonder of

God," spoke the angel.

Paul had slowly gained his balance and could recall the events of the past hour. *Why can't I cross into a place of peace and quiet?* He was no longer a pawn in this series of events. He followed his advocate to a place that looked into Iowa from a higher elevation.

The angel returned quickly to his light form, but now was surrounded by hundreds of holy warriors with swords and staves. Their armor was brilliant and made of solid gold.

"I will remove the shackles from your eye, Paul. You will see what I see, and hear what I hear," said the angel. He then motioned his hand in a slight wave across Paul's face.

"Look and see, my friend."

A horde of many demons redirected their vision and headed straight toward Paul. They were hissing and growling and yelling blasphemous insults. Their numbers appeared countless.

The holy host adamantly stood, prevailing against the assaults. Those that fell were replaced by any number of fearless warriors. The demons challenged, driven by a more maleficent host, yet they failed. Nothing living or dead could lead them successfully against the angels.

"Do not allow this to cause you concern," said Paul's protecting angel. "Those evil ones must destroy you at all costs and will continue this assault until you return to your human form. Their momentary existence, they believe, is sustained by their quest to halt the completion of God's plan. They haven't the ability to discern that they were dead when they came into existence. The dimension that prevented you from entering is now momentarily open to you. You may not enter, but you can speak for a short time with anyone you chose. Just call them and they will be here."

"Mom. Dad," Paul called, and they stood before him, smiling and laughing. "How have you been?" he asked.

"We are well, my son. We are preparing a place for you when your time has ended. Take care and be of good faith. We will hope to be together soon," responded his mother. With that, they walked away toward a breathless place that could not be described.

He wanted to run to them and hold them, but was encumbered by the angel. "One more," he cautioned, "because your form is beginning to fade."

The warriors continued their steadfast duty, while slaying the unholy foe and driving them back into the abyss.

"Lena!" She did not appear. "Lena!" Tears filled his eyes, and he sought to secretly wipe them away. *Where are you, my love?* he asked himself.

The angel responded, "She is not here." "Where then?"

"She lies across a big valley held in momentary stasis until the time of human reign on earth has ended and God judges all. When those who have died by their own hands will be judged according to their deeds. The Lord is most forgiving."

"Can we go there now?" asked Paul.

"We cannot, because you have another journey that you must take."

"Please, go get her."

"I cannot."

Paul could not see the battle that was occurring all around him, but he did notice the yellow grain fields around him, the roads, and the few trees in the area.

"Let us go," said the angel. The angel motioned him into the mist, and reluctantly he went. They emerged in what appeared to be a land that was not arid. The weather was warm and temperate. The brightness reflected the light of the sun that shone brightly.

"Where are we?" asked Paul, inwardly hoping that he had been escorted to the valley where his love, Lena, would be.

"We are in Axum, Ethiopia, and are standing in front of St. Mary of Zion Church. Come with me." The angel resumed his human form.

They walked to the door and knocked. An elderly man greeted them and bowed. "Welcome, my lord," said the priest.

"Rise, faithful servant. The Lord is well pleased with your duty."

"I am honored," he replied with lowered eyes.

"This is Paul, your brother," said the angel. "Show us your gift."

"Enter, honored host sent from God. Behold."

Paul stumbled backward. *Is this really the Arc of the Covenant?*

"Please stand," said the angelic host. He reached out to help the priest.

The Arc of the Covenant, in all its glory, stood before him. It glowed in a profound brightness that startled the priest and Paul. A loud thundering voice that forced Paul backward, then to his knees, and the Ethiopian priest to the ground, engulfed the room. "Fear not for this is the Alpha and the Omega, your God. Your time is not yet, but be assured, in you I am well pleased. I have more for you to do, this will be much more trying, the purest evil now awaits you. I will be with you always. Great power and knowledge will be at your only wish. Stand firm."

The voice and radiance passed as the room returned to its previous state. There were many thoughts running through Paul's head, but none found a way out.

"Please stand." He reached out to help the priest. The angel then assisted Paul. "This begins the Time of Sorrow, spoken of in Daniel. The Time of Tribulations are upon you."

CHAPTER 59

Paul waited patiently in his Nissan Altima, watching the clouds that had suddenly arrived. The wind immediately followed, suggesting that they would soon release its fury upon the area. There were ominous black and gray clouds shielding the afternoon sun that shone brightly outside the area that lay below them.

It was not unusual to have these afternoon showers in this tropical weather pattern that had lingered for days. Paul peered around, wondering why people had not sought shelter when this act repeated itself over and over. Those walking occasionally searched the skies but lacked any increased desire to avoid the imminent threatening weather. The trees were withering against the wild wind and fought the assaulting weather.

Laughing, Paul watched the people scurry for cover as the rain assaulted them. It was a blinding, biting rain. Hastily assembled umbrellas swept across the roads and slammed into anything in their way. What were they thinking? They had to know that the torrential rain was going to unleash its fury. Maybe they wanted to be cooled and soaked. Paul had no idea. He still thought it was funny.

As soon as the rain came, it departed. The blue sky in all its glory reclaimed the sky. Washington Avenue in Alexandria, Virginia, was still Washington Avenue. Looking out at the diminishing rainfall that was abruptly ending, Paul parked along Church Street gazing at St. Mary's cemetery. Three years had passed since the battle with the frenzy demonic hoard. There had not been contact with either the guardian angel or the minions of the underworld.

Headstones of every type and size filled the graveyard, which was over three centuries in existence. Most of the headstones were oval, but some stretched over six feet tall. Most were dulled by time, wear, and tear. A few were enclosed with iron gates, segregating them from the others. A few black granite stones were intermingled among the cemetery.

Walking through the cemetery, Paul was cognizant of the area where stones were placed and the interred rested. He did not want to walk on them. He avoided the fallen. Emotions arose in his mind, which troubled his spirit. His parents, best friend, and former girlfriend rested here. He was visiting them after three years to pay respect and recall a better emotional time.

There were others walking and mumbling to lifeless granite stones. All of the visitors were there for a similar purpose. They shared thoughts of a better time. Paul was trampling the manicured grass while attempting to not interfere with graves. He bent down at his girlfriend's grave but lacked any good memories, no fond memories. Death and darkness overwhelmed him. He abruptly stood.

Glaring upward, he looked skyward, gasping for a breath. His heart appeared to beat quicker, and his chest expanded. Excitement and worry battled for prominence in his thoughts, and he suddenly recalled the previous years.

Four unmounted horses, taller than any horse he had ever witnessed, gazed toward him. The colors of the horses were black, white, red, and pale, with eyes glaring crimson red. They stood like fierce steel awaiting their riders, who soon appeared with instruments of death, readying for war. Paul watched the riders mount the horses in unison as they whinnied and neighed. They were preparing for battle.

As the vision faded, Paul awaited the angel who had assisted him through his previous ordeal. He looked around and stared toward others at the cemetery. No acknowledgment came; no one spoke to him. Certainly, that vision was for him. He ended his visit. *What does the vision mean?* he asked himself. *When will someone provide the answers?*

ABOUT THE AUTHOR

Leanear Randall was born in Washington, DC. He served twenty-seven years in the United States Army. While in the Army, he earned numerous military and civilian awards. Leanear is an accomplished martial artist with over fifty years of researching, teaching, and practicing Goju-ryu martial arts.